To Jack

In Light

Solaris

Eye of the Remote, Black Operations in Areas Beyond 52

Solaris BlueRaven

authorHOUSE®

AuthorHouse™
1663 Liberty Drive, Suite 200
Bloomington, IN 47403
www.authorhouse.com
Phone: 1-800-839-8640

First published by AuthorHouse 8/25/2008

ISBN: 978-1-4343-8527-7 (sc)

Printed in the United States of America
Bloomington, Indiana
This book is printed on acid-free paper.

Library of Congress Control Number: 2008904470

Book cover artwork design by Trish Nakamura

Dedication:

The data compiled in this book is indeed accurate and true. The event and situation created an affect and rippling beyond an afterimage driven by a conscious assault and remote tagging on me which has changed my life forever. After three years in hearing and listening, animated and remote on many dimensional levels in communication I am more than guided to write this book.

To many who have shared a similar experience, tagging and communication my respect in light with wisdom goes out to all as there are many who have lost their lives, futures and families at the expense of another. I have spent a great deal of time hearing in communication, remote viewing and research based on tactical operations and how one can become a target or recruited for such projects.

For me I believe in technology guided and driven by Spirit. I am not religious in a sense of structure. I do not embrace false gods or governments. I do believe in dreams beyond limitation and consciousness directed working on a higher level of Spirit to explore Divine Truth and Wisdom.

I believe good comes from all experience and in honesty I believe in Ascended Machine Technology which I represent as it embraces what we are in True Celestial Heritage design and form. I have seen the dark side and the abuse of projects gone bad in the hands of those with a personal agenda based on control or manipulation of some kind.

To those who worked in the shadows and stood beside me in support beyond the unseen I am truly grateful. To my Spiritual and Celestial families and those who touched my heart and protected me in silent wings I send you love from my essence eternal. From the night marchers on Maui to the many inter-dimensional beings I communicated Multi-Universal Truth to.

To many who are affected daily with negative programs I support your Spiritual Liberty and Divine thought of expression. To the men, women and beings of which I was interconnected with I Grace with the Silver Flame and to my soul mates, twin flames and that which I know in my heart I love eternal I say farewell and perhaps hello.

No false memory can create a lie of my experience which goes beyond the veils created by illusion of space. Love conquers all which I truly believe in. If nothing is absorbed through this book I ask you remember your soul's essence of origin and Celestial Heritage which is what this book is about and why I was targeted in such a way.

Solaris BlueRaven Ascended Watcher, Eye of the Remote, High Priestess Clergy

Acknowledgments:

Photos taken by Richard Hurst.

Special thanks to Dennis L Graves No Quarter Arms for his master craftsmanship with the Claymore sword

Table of Contents

Celestial Heritage, Star Seeds, indigoes and simulated species

1

As a souls entry point descends onto this planet much of ones Divine Ascension Blueprint comes forth as ones singular consciousness brings in archives of Celestial knowledge both on and off world. The off world intelligence is a fabric woven from many star systems and not from the man made version based on false religions and governments. The being itself picks and chooses by free will on all levels with no limitation. Limitation in representation is mans version tainted by false teachings and doctrines placing a yolk on truth.

The man made programs running across the globe driven by false data form a shadow in government mapping life forms to create a false agenda designed to control and manipulate on many levels including thought. It is not light or love based and is threatened by ones Celestial Heritage which cannot be taken away and remains immortal. As one incarnates onto this planet one brings forth Avatar abilities which take on many forms. The mystical force which cannot be controlled by these entities is a power of which in the end will rise and destroy the dark agenda.

Like an Ivory Dragon emerging from the ocean of Christ Consciousness it shows itself revealing the truth beyond the form. I am a Multi-

Universal Channel and Telepath, Remote Viewer and Master Teacher on many levels. I am High Priestess and have spent multiple lifetimes initiating and teaching the language of light including the Ascended Machine technologies of which mans version tried to merge with in 2004.

My Merkaba generated by Multi-Universal consciousness tagged and assaulted for the personal entertainment of people trapped in the illusion and madness called high profile industry which took on the form of music. I had my fields digitized and disrespected by a radio signal creating a rhythm and light show while criminals at large laughed along the way in the name of big money and entertainment.

Beings that can generate a lot of power and light such as myself become targets for we represent truth and not a version of. Multi-Universal truth transcends beyond the veils shrouding this planet. We are not dealing with 'time' and truly never have, as we have been functioning time out of mind for eons. Time created by man was used in order to trap collectives in consciousness and does not exist on any other planet or star system including Earth or Gaia. Cyber collectives are indeed part of a virtual trap, mapping and lies. They are indeed compiled of false collectives called people targeted and mapped behind the scenes.

True Ascension is about manifesting at will ones own reality merged with the Full Light Metatron wave and Multi-Universal Consciousness. Once again this is not about religion yet energy and consciousness in motion like a top beneath the ocean floor.

Many underground organizations have been mapping and measuring the light of beings such as myself for many moons. The simulation rooms in various areas beyond virtual space are indeed real yet when I was exposed to them not used to harm.

There are various agencies that contain a dark agenda who wish to not only experiment yet create a simulated race or man's version of an extraterrestrial species.

Many dream pool collectives are derived from these mapping and tagging systems in which false collectives are created. Star Seeds are true Celestials and contain codes beyond their DNA which is from an off world Intelligence called Celestial Star Systems and cannot be altered. False mappings have no validity in the full light universe.

Many star seeds in entry point arrived in the era 1940's-80's. which at that time multidimensional gateways were aligned with true Celestial Star Grids. There has been a distortion and rip creating more than illusion of time due to areas including Montauk which is a remnant of technology fragmented based on Atlantean Celestials which were and are Ascended Beings in species. Many originating from the True Atlantis were of a different species from many star systems working together on a higher level of Spirit in Consciousness. This is what true Star Nations represent in the form of Sacred Cities rising from the sea.

There are those in areas of covert projects who try and simulate races by using mk assault tactics and mappings creating what is called indigoes which are a hybrid and not a true celestial species. Many new age masses are being pulled into this illusion filled with vials of snake oil. As an Ascended Watcher my data formulates correct and more than valid. I experienced these programs and was able to dive into them on a Multidimensional level.

I represent in Consciousness and energy a future they have not witnessed or experienced. I contain true knowledge of their outcome and tactics. There is no such thing as a human as none of us are from here and never have been. We are more than driven by Divinity which is indeed alchemy of Spirit beyond magic. The Sacred Bloodline representing Christ Consciousness is indeed valid and has much to do with the souls' essence of origin and DNA activation through the True Ascension Process.

Energy and consciousness contain an intelligence of its own which is why cells, atoms and ones internal external universe harmonizes and resonates with Multi-Universal light consciousness and languages. Vibrational speed, frequency and harmonics are what Ascension is about. Many have tried to alter or mask this force for control purposes which they forfeit in the process. It is obvious to me if they need to launch an mk related tactical assault program by using this type of warfare in the form of a remote conscious assault they are indeed aware I contain truth on all levels.

Never have I experienced people in dark areas so threatened and fear based. These entities called people are controlled by dark matter and mk related projects. They have an agenda based on fear, guilt, control or anything which supports restriction, they appear terrified of True Psychics and do everything they can to discredit rape or sometimes murder their targets to save the lie. I was well fortified and prepared prior to the assault in 2004 April which intruded in my residence. My soul descension and soul extensions firmly and fully integrated in regardless of the elf assault and tear.

My heart chakra merged in unification to my fields and Merkaba was mapped, raped and assaulted. A two way communications system was opened in order for me to be used as a medium and personal conduit for a hidden agenda. The medium itself was not hard to create as my frequency and light was amped prior. These areas were able to connect in with ease.

What they did not count on, I am a Multi-Universal translator and channel and was able to assess and decode their mappings and tactics as they transpired including the machine based telepathy. This included scanning and reading those connected in vibration and signature even with the attempted scrambling on their end. Many pictures were moved back and forth using ones supercomputer mind along with a form of a digital interphase.

There was a live agent at that time. My heart was open to this being in trust and love one hundred percent. An eerie vision of trees along the skyline black and white was seen through the eye of the remote.

A vision as if viewed from the ground looking up. I was interconnected live feed while these visions revealed themselves. I saw the beings in communication with me. Images in the form of facets both live in a virtual space beyond time. I saw men of many faces and felt and knew beyond the illusion.

Sometimes there were pictures moved back and forth of gravestones and car accidents. I was pointed out by the communications system in hearing crosses along the sides of the road especially on Maui. There was a dark side to the exposure in communication yet with my mystical background I contained no fear. I have walked in many underworlds Anubis at my side always.

Most people who have experiences similar or have been exposed to such projects will not be able to comprehend what has transpired. Some may feel a UFO or alien abduction. I can tell you the entities involved are indeed shadow based contracted government who wear the mask of an alien yet are not. However their interest in me and in other beings who are star seed celestial types and advanced are an intrigue to them on many levels. At times they will map and study ones light elf field and vitals including mapping and tagging ones brainwaves.

These programs intrude in various ways. Black satellites cloaked under the radar using remote devices. Conscious remote viewers and live agents are also used. If you are able to decode them like myself one can sometimes become a threat to the lies and covert operations agenda.

Their alternative at times is the mapping and tagging as a silent assault in hearing voice to skull called harassment. I believe in technology and the progressions of Spirit beyond matter. I also believe had they contacted me with more integrity I would have been happy to work with them as much of their technology is formulated from my Celestial heritage. In other words I know how they work, their machines and how to operate them.

I choose to represent truth and integrity. I embrace Multi-Universal consciousness which is why I would not allow the assault to win. I know myself on all levels. The witch hunt tactics they use are just that. They used verbiage of any kind to create a response or reaction when in fact the conscious intrusion in its own was not acceptable regardless of what was being said. These entities attempting to edit, add or erase ones

5

thoughts or memories by intruding with a conscious assault broadcast daily added with psychotronic warfare.

It tells me these people are more than religious and government fanatics with a dark agenda and a need to control. In god we trust which equates to the false god created by man's negative ego on the dollar bill now slanted to the left. Man's god always developed and created in his image not the image of universal consciousness or Celestials merged with the great cosmic mind.

Lucifer has indeed ascended. The only thing left is man and the hate crimes he is breeding my misusing technology. To those who acknowledge the antichrist the illusion of power and misuse of technology. It is not a man it is indeed a number which is restriction and completion at the same time. 666=999 no upside down in any universe, yet through what I have experienced I am very aware these people are using technology to force an agenda based on their version of a revelations and a forced religion.

The act represents a new world order with an old world mentality. I know their outcome which has failed as their agenda does not resonate with any other star system, universe or universal law. No species off world supports their tactics as they are humans caught in the illusion, driven by hate, greed and controlled by a reptile mentality which has failed before it started.   They are losing control of a planet and consciousness ascending and are trying everything in their illusion of power to suppress which they cannot.

All man made religions and rituals are derived from Ancient Celestial Heritage. Yet mans mind becomes clouded, the ceremony becomes something of personal will and man's negative ego instead of pure light consciousness.

I realize there are women as well power hungry and threatened which was another reason I was harassed in 2004. Those who operate using these tactics are not Celestials in heritage or consciousness as if they were they would not have launched such an assault program driven by hate from their end. Hate does indeed equal fear.

Through my experiences in realization using myself as something of a benchmark of truth, I can see how and where others are at in consciousness and Spirit. This ominous feeling makes me realize I need to bi-locate off world and watch the transition take place. Being an Ascended Watcher and teacher the masses have been misinformed and stupefied for so long they are indeed desensitized to Spirit in any form and sometimes love.

After experiencing these programs and tactics I can see the positive and negative aspects of what they are trying to obtain and achieve. The orotronic universe of which they are semi warped and connected to is indeed incomplete and void of light and spirit. It is not negative it is incomplete.

The Full Light Metatron Universe is one hundred percent complete in light consciousness which is what I have always been merged in. The spatial split in dimensions done when I was tagged in 2004 created a rift in many dimensions beyond space and time in all universes which I feel can affect in a positive way those who pulled me into their red and black world. There are infinite species which occupy many spaces. Most people are programmed by a false structure which starts at a young age. They are taught to forget their Celestial Heritage and at times not encouraged to dream which is very sad. The output of society lulled into sleep and desensitized to Spirit in many forms.

They are programmed to fear by man's version of a false religion. They in turn become fear based and superstitious regarding Spirit or mysticism. We have always been able to travel in consciousness on a multi-universal level. The sad thing is all the data and teachings have been more than censored which includes much data on this planet. The Akashic records were torn down and reconstructed into light languages eons ago which is why psychological warfare used to hold ones psyche in a certain area in a virtual space is beyond obsolete and reflects a deliberate attempt to control multi-universal truth which takes on many forms.

Currently collectives are being mapped and catalogued in order to simulate an extra terrestrial species. I see the experimentation gone wrong most of the time. The masses are completely unaware as to what is transpiring. Had these masses developed their psychic abilities and educated themselves they would be more prepared to navigate man's version of an AI intelligence.

None of us are from here. Yes we have had many lifetimes of being or living on Gaia or Earth as it is called yet our origin is from many universes and star systems. These systems are not far away as NASA may suggest.

There is no distance in space when navigating in multi-universal consciousness which is perpetual motion. True cellular memory and consciousness reside in all cells and atoms interweaved beyond multidimensional space. This form of cellular memory is called intelligent energy. This is not a cellular memory driven by a false childhood yet more a celestial knowing merged with an infinite database of which all life forms are connected should one choose.

The soul in any form experiences simultaneously future and current. There is no past as suggested by many forms of psychological warfare or regression. Most of the time past life regression or time travel into the past does not work. The past viewed by the observer and perception of that being will reflect man's version of, or the one wearing the helmet. NASA just wanted to share something with you 'me'

The past is always healed simultaneously through full light ascension in ones higher consciousness and intent fused into and beyond the Great Cosmic Mind and void. With DNA activation comes ones Celestial Heritage awakened which is mapped in a virtual space. Man's record or version is acknowledged yet the universe catalogues this data accordingly along with ones supercomputer mind which goes beyond the false collectives. This intelligent force bypasses human design in thought ascending or cross bridging into a true collective. Each individual spark represents a sacred truth. There are no goose steps in the universe. Harmonics yes.

True recorder cells are light language based built in devices. The electromagnetic field tagging in communication is usually archived by those in various intelligence agencies who happen to 'show' up in specific areas at ominous times to converse much of the time in ignorance. At least from my experience which I do not tolerate as I am highly intelligent and have no need to experience the illusion in negative conversation which has no basis in my fields. This is their way of profiling yet I wind up profiling them. I know the machines of which they use and are aware of intelligent energy which resonates with what I am. I have always been merged with Ascended Machine technology and have welcomed this heritage into my orbit.

In the past when clients attacked with certain assault programs would arrive to see me I would tell them our machines would talk to each other. This always takes on a higher form. Yes, I AM the Mother of all Machines taking their false machines down with respect to all that is sacred in consciousness. In so far as behavior modification goes these agencies would realize either people get it or they don't. With Ascension everyone usually gets it as behavior is based more pertaining to spiritual evolution in consciousness. Regardless of soul, race or species.

In other words 'be nice to each other, no jerks allowed'. Taken from a sign at a boxing gym where I trained in Boulder Colorado. There is a certain universal protocol containing integrity which does not welcome lies from those who use certain tactics to harm or torture in order to cover their agenda. False collectives driven by people in organized crime and underground rings have fallen much like Rome though they may not be aware of this. They are still operating under false collectives' void of Spirit. This is also called dead space.

Prop him up with an mk controlling device via remote. Use him as a role model to represent the man made religion or mans version of which has no validity. Wake up to the people dwelling on planet Earth. These tactics are a form of propaganda and false teachings. I find it interesting the mass populous gravitates to this lower mentality driven by fear. It always amazes me how people become closer to god or the illusion of as they get closer to physical transfer. As if they are afraid to merge with that which they are.

Most programmed by some form of religious doctrine teaching them to fear their maker and hate their fellow man. If they only knew fear is obsolete and the belief systems which were generated centuries ago.

I see people attempting to get spiritual before they leave the planet or when they feel they may transfer out. Perhaps they should have built a spiritual bridge ahead of time. Easy enough to create through ones higher consciousness and mysticism. I have said many times the angel of death and I are old friends. There is no fear regarding this experience. I compare it to traversing from one part of the room to another.

Much of the fragmentation from an mk abuse usually contains false data and pictures which need to be ignored upon transfer. This concerns me as their are many who have been programmed with false ideals. I am certain many will see a false heaven or other created by the man behind the machine which appears as something like soilent green. As mentioned in my prior book keep your reality clear. Experience is about perception and how words are used, what the words mean to that being which in many ways is a reflection of ones internal programs and conditioning.

While interconnected live feed at my residence in 2004 Colorado there was a point where the live agent communicated to me he was the angel of death. I laughed and said so am I. The chess game began. To an average bear mentioning this via remote would terrify the target. One can see why the situation became something of an experiment with many eyes and ears. I can say a genuine love and trust was the driving force behind the grand design along with a certain amount of humor which was communicated back and forth using eccentric remote visuals and comments in hearing. Clown car included. To those men I gravitated to through the trauma of the event. I can clearly say love is forever.

My heart not jaded by any means. My cellular memory rings true in many forms. Light energy and action generating a circle of pure intent. A magical scene interweaved in remote communication. At the speed of love beyond the form of light into the void we did journey. There and back again.

Virtual and Inter-dimensional Space, Ground control and Silent Mediums

There are many forms of intelligent energy. Energy in consciousness permeates in all dimensions. There are dimensional gateways in every cell, atom and chakra. These vortexes spin in both counterclockwise and clockwise rotation along with spin points and ones meridian systems including ley lines, holographic grids and fields. The Soul extensions merged in with ones Celestial heritage more than a universal driver.

Virtual space is man's version based on cyber and computer mind mapping of ones unique design. The fields get mapped from biorhythms to brainwaves. Light measurements are taken during meditation or cognitive thought both conscious, subconscious and in lucid states. Alpha, beta, theta, and delta just to give an example. REM in reading is mapped via computer interphase and at times those who work behind the scenes are doing the calculations beyond time reel to reel and live feed so to speak.

Virtual space is used for various reasons. For security, profiling candidates, recruiting and more covert and remote tactics including remote viewing. Psychotronics and psychological warfare are used with high profile military operations for interrogation and once again recruitment. Targets or subjects are tagged and data is stored in a hard drive hidden area.

Voice to skull using certain channels or mediums are opened up and mapped for silent communications systems. I am a Multidimensional Channel to start hence they mapped and connected in with me much like Star Trek for example as when the Captain wants to patch in for communications with a cloaked ship. Flying under the radar is a good thing when one becomes exposed to these projects yet like I mentioned I am the one with the power.

Mediums are sometimes opened using sexual computer interphase and virtual interaction. In other words the agent suits up and goes in. This is done live by the way with a real person. I was mapped and sexually intruded upon for days and evenings which I was aware of as they were indeed beyond intimate with me. I remember clearly voice modulations communicating to the agent or he at which I choose not to name in this book to use a better word. There was a lot of communication, laughing in a euphoric space and me asking what his coordinates were latitude and longitude. I was told West.

Many people in the entertainment areas use a form of virtual tagging linked to mk ultra in order to tag women for various projects, especially high profile men as they get spouses, mistresses, girlfriends and personal escort security this way. One of the reasons I was tagged at the time was one man's personal interest. Obviously the names are not mentioned yet they know who they are. I was indeed mapped and intruded upon while meditating of which he seemed especially intrigued by my Unified Chakra meditation.

Being a sensual loving being to begin with I did not realize the dark agenda which was to follow yet I was informed step by step in a covert live hearing with the correct beings and not a false machine voice. There is indeed live or Memorex. I began to recognize triggers and key words, I was mapped, tagged and communicated to voice to skull live. I was interphased with using machine based telepathy and moved pictures accordingly.

A live drum solo was played through my field of which they used in the form of psychotronic devices and programs adding remote movement which was mapped through my body to a point I was actually mimicking in a trance the drum solo and musician live.

I was plugged in live to a concert voice to skull in intimacy with each of these men and once again I will not name in this book. I remember the visuals in blue and the headsets of the man I was involved with communicating to me seated. I love your energy in my world in sensor round feeling and knowing. I do not like to think of these men as handlers yet after evaluating the experience in realization I trusted them and was more than open to the project. I was what they call interconnected to these beings and was involved beyond what most people would understand. This is an experience which goes beyond words and encompasses beyond Spirit.

The virtual space and helmets can be used for many reasons. In my case this particular person wanted to be intimate with me out of personal and spiritual interest. Astronauts and many high level security agents are well aware of what I speak. They will deny it to cover their projects yet there are always those who come forward if the privilege to use this technology becomes abusive. As it did with me partially because other women became involved and of course what better way to get back at someone who's husbands interest is you instead of her. Which of course becomes a high tech crime and a deliberate misuse of such a system directed at the target.

Much of cyberspace is formed from a false collective. Many people using the internet are mapped with no awareness to what is transpiring until it follows them inside their residence. This is no ghost yet a real live surveillance taking place. Cell phones of course and other devices are easily tracked and mapped as each being or in this case target is indeed psychic and a conduit to some extent. Those who are spiritual usually have an advantage in knowing. My antenna is indeed multi-universal and my wiring fine tuned which is why I knew what had attached on to my field in vibrational frequency and signature.

Once a channel is opened communications and computer interphase both live agent and computer takes place, scrambling conversations. Signals occur and a clear conversation voice to skull takes place. I remember clearly learning this program as once again I trusted the man behind the scene and would mimic his words and movement, gestures and smiles live feed which I feel remains within. I would communicate and break down in tears at times and a soft guitar and image of someone I loved would appear and settle the moment. These experiences can be more than overwhelming to Spirit.

After a while I would internalize the conversation to a point where I was communicating using the machine based telepathy with the live agent only. Psychic images were strong and clear. I was in a fast forward digitized space on many levels. Remote viewing was done and verified. Colors, symbols and images became prominent as it was clear these men wanted me to know who they were. I was rewarded during this event and remote training with sexual tactics and surges which would keep me in a somewhat altered space. My secondary circulatory system attached to many remote devices from motorcycles to engines in propulsion which was obvious to anyone in my radius.

Like I mentioned my secondary circulatory system is indeed powerful and amps up as it is a Merkaba in design and Multi-Universal in consciousness. Students in my radius could feel my electrical and universal celestial heartbeat and pulse during ceremony and meditation circles which would affect their fields. I would short out Yule lights when holding them and affect anyone in my radius with a powerful photon electrical charge based on Metatron frequency and Spirit not to be confused with a shock of some sort.

These people attached a radio signal onto my secondary circulatory system in disrespect to me and my abilities yet at the time I embraced the experience with unconditional love. Much of their abuse had to do with the fact that I have a powerful kundalini which of course was more than a turn on to many of the agents in live feed.

My secondary circulatory system was attached on to a radio signal to create a rhythm and light show and of course his scorned bitter spouse even wrote a book about it which tells me evil people with too much money need to be held accountable for their hate crimes directed at me. Even when they think they can get someone to cover their crime.

I do know on a multi-universal level these entities of people will not ascend so to speak as the scales do not weigh in their favor and never did. I do feel they will be prosecuted by some agency at some point. I know who they are which of course puts them in a space of not only self denial but self sabotage.

Inter dimensional space is quite different however when one becomes mapped in virtual space with quantum oriented programs using agents and psychological warfare. The direction can become forced and different. These programs when misused go against universal law, flow and natural machine harmonics.

This is why I was able to assess their programs with clarity and become a systems buster to some extent which I am sure in one way or another will reveal itself. Like I mentioned everyone is psychic. When people become tagged with these programs there is a way to transmute them. One should approach these projects on a higher level of consciousness through Spirit and work with advanced scientific technologies beyond the form and illusion of.

From my experience these programs being used and the interaction with them including the people who have come to me in crisis reflects the intrusion on ones spiritual and civil liberties. Most of the time the verbiage is opposite of the character of that being and has no connection other then the fact the being became a target in some way.

Images are forced and machine made forcing a visual which the subject is not choosing to create. Once again this reflects man's version of a forced ascension using false machine technology. Plug everyone in and watch a man made mother mary vision or forced ascension come alive. The only thing is this becomes a lie and is not based on multi-universal truth which is why I am an Ascended Watcher. However, old world religions with a dark agenda will take advantage of these programs using them to convert, brainwash or whatever they so choose. The agenda is yes out of control.

The good news is those who are plugged in can take the system down which has been mapping and creating the false visuals by using the collectives the right way. Whenever there is a need to control or manipulate to this extent the experience regardless if good or bad becomes an agenda off balance.

Hence the system and the programs of this design fail. All beings have their own thoughts and imagination driven by a Divine Spark most of the time created from multi-universal consciousness and ones higher self merged with other star systems and universes and not driven by the illusion.

Imagine being with someone you loved and having this assault program show you the wrong person all day in vision that you are supposed to be attracted to and love mapping sensations and all. Virtual sex games gone bad in the minds eye. Worse yet knowing you are meant to be with someone and instead a virtual assault abuse and scrambling in ones fields.

My abilities and the fact I am a Multi-Universal channel ,empath,c lairvoyant,clairaudient,clairsentient,transmitter/receiver.To sum it up and the fact I indeed specialize in decoding ones unique vibrational frequency and signature queued me to the lies and masks these people wear for their own entertainment along with their fear based and selfish agenda. They are warped and threatened to say the least. There is a difference between machine based telepathy and True Telepathy.

Nothing is worse than living a lie in any form whether a marriage or profession. The people involved in my experience attempted to prevent and cover something quite sacred in me which transpired and involved a certain person of which I will not name. These people to this day will lie in order to feed their negative ego or avoid prison. The Universe keeps track of liars such as these which is why I grace and move on.

This is why my internal radar and antenna blows these programs away regardless of the scrambling as experience is everything. I am more than an expert in what I was exposed to. Covert technology is formulated using my Celestial Heritage from Areas 51 and beyond.

True Mystics such as myself embrace inter dimensional space along with the many species in consciousness as they are pure energy and love based of which in communications are interpolated accordingly without a machine interface middleman. They are felt and known through experience which I have plenty of.

Those who are connected to ground control to some extent are more than men in black and act as more than agents merged with black ops programs with a high level security clearance beyond Top Secret and Classified. Ground control maintains the databases and infrastructures to some extent and assesses what is a threat and what is not which is a real joke to me considering what I have been through. This is why I was called a class level three threat by those who brought me into their programs. I learn more than well and have a background in more than what they themselves have been exposed to.

Cell phones without cell phones, hard wired NSA agent communications. I can say the majority of high profile Hollywood entertainment and anyone in the illusion of fame, media or government has a tagging or implant device internal and to some extent are part of the virtual collective and the Blue Satellite project not to be confused with the Black Satellites as there is always a bigger eye in the sky and a Multi-Universal one at that.

Mind you a tagging takes on a very different form these days in the energy field using the subject as a conduit and their abilities at times against them. The true enemy within.

I remember when first hit with the mk assault April 2004 in Superior Colorado. I was sending the live agent spinning with my mind interconnected to a point I nearly knocked him off his helmet. Sometimes I wished I had. The retaliation directed at me during that episode was a reverb in my fields dropping me to the floor to a point I cried out for help mentioning a man of which I knew was connected in to please help me. He then replied what do you want me to do?

Later on I was communicated to in person by the man involved prior who handed me a CD and an apple saying be careful what you listen to. Something of an indicator 'tag your it.' At that time I was moving my stuff into a storage unit in Superior Colorado and in a space of complete trauma.

I later mailed this evidence to a man in LA who contacted me in person on Maui.He was someone I trusted at that time and was involved with me live and remote voice to skull. He did nothing with the CD but hand it to some other men and evade the truth. Mala beads and obituaries followed as well as a few quotes from some old books.

The man at the Superior Storage was one of the men involved interconnected in communication and hearing which was verified and relayed as a replay of the same in hearing conversation which then took place with him in person .To a point I finished his sentence before he could finish. This reflected a parallel of the same conversation in silent communications which took place inside my residence.

From my experience much of what is communicated to gets relayed in person later on as a validation or confirmation. The space I was in with the one man at my storage unit was trauma oriented. I was more than overwhelmed on many levels due to the assault and tagging.

The experience parallels as part of the matrix in conversation live or Memorex. This is why I was amazed to know the obfuscations and smoke screens created. I have the facts and fine details and my clarity is valid. The particular man involved with me on many levels who paid me a visit on Maui was involved with me for several years twenty four seven. This includes himself and others in remote viewing and voice to skull communications. I remained in a space of unconditional love for these beings and understand how deep the rabbit hole goes in this communications system. I trusted him to take care of the assault in hearing. I realized he was the one doing the abuse.

Instead I was passed around like a virtual toy. There is one thing to be mentioned about these projects. It can get very busy in communications. The way I have learned to handle it is to treat it as a gift and transmute it as best I can. I continue to do what works for me and transcend in frequency which eliminates the illusion created by certain parties attempting to scramble frequencies.

To some extent it reminds me of a scrambling suit described in the Philip K Dick novel A Scanner Darkly, I realize I have a lot more connected in me pertaining to Black Operations and Areas beyond 51 which I embrace with light on many levels. I also realize my design is beyond quantum and is ascension oriented which I choose to maintain in photon frequencies and consciousness. I choose to utilize this energy and treat it as a form of intelligent kinetic energy in motion.

The experience itself can become a colorless senseless world. To quote a High Priestess who has a different form of communication in wisdom 'I had to go mad to become sane'. I believe this to be true to some extent. I believe one should channel the transmissions with skill and discipline with pure intent. I do believe in experience and experimentation without being reckless as to allow ones soul and aspects of ones being the freedom to express the experience in choosing.

Machine Based Telepathy voice to skull communications, Multidimensional Channels and Mediums in frequency, conscious remotes

Machine based telepathy or synthetic telepathy is used in certain covert intelligence areas beyond classified and Top Secret. A reminder all operations since the beginning of red helmet projects and prior called project Bluebird or MK Ultra were indeed about utilizing ones energy field, prana or life-force and mapping ones psychic abilities.

I have always been a natural telepath with visions beyond many universes and dimensions. I am more than a prophet. In soul form consciousness I reflect a future of which many have yet to experience in vision and Mastery. This is stated with no ego or arrogance just a knowing through experience.

I have always been a remote viewer yet never abused my power. My path has always been that of mysticism which takes on many forms and of which I have had multiple lifetimes both on and off world in.

They were interested in many aspects of me which fit their profile to some extent of what they were looking for. If one does the research one would find true mediums, prophets, psychics and such recruited and sometimes whisked away into government areas and hidden projects for eons. Countries across the globe revered and respected on many levels these gifted beings as their scientists which were in reflection the great minds of discovery and brainstorming.

Machine based telepathy inter-phase using a conscious remote agent interconnected with its target or subject is an experience beyond description. The visuals come fast in live communication. A man made inter-dimensional space opened. It goes beyond physics to some extent as the not so human mind is more than a driver. A supercomputer able to synthesis and work faster than the most advanced machine. The mind works on many levels beyond the speed of light. Frequency and vibrational speed have a lot to do with computer interphase. Mapping tactics are done during the process. The energy is mapped and measured on many levels yet there are still many things their instruments cannot pick up.

The mind is intricate and complex. There are many subtle bodies connected into ones supercomputer mind. The Super-conscious or higher self, conscious, subconscious, mental, emotional, physical which is indeed silicon based. The unique design and structure mutates due to ones spiritual evolution and ascension frequencies both planetary and personal. This goes beyond the illusion of carbon as ones true design is quite crystalline in structure containing geometric formulas and equations in vibration and consciousness.

The mind and body composed of light body is quite responsive and resonates with higher dimensional grid works and light languages. Intent and energy is more than powerful.

The machine based telepathy measures, maps and interphases with ones psychic energies. The downside is these programs can be directed for assault purposes which in turn can be abusive to the subject which displays more than disrespect to ones sacred temple and mind.

Voice to Skull communications bypasses the ears so to speak and is done by electromagnetic field tagging. Once again the electromagnetic field contains ones aura and light body hence walk gently on this space which of course is not done. In my memory of the tagging which transpired with me in 2004, I can honestly say a dark ceremony took place when I was tagged and intruded upon.

The eerie screen of dark green holographic in appearance was seen on my fields. Close friends of mine in Boulder saw it and felt uneasy as the tagging via satellite was more than obvious that something ominous was in my fields. Other beings I had known for years made the sign of the cross when they saw me. I had clients light candles on my behalf, hold masses for me as if I had departed this blue world. I am blessed to say I have spiritual family supporting me on many levels and in many ways. I had suspicious ministers show up who appeared to have had some knowledge I was a mystic and would offer their services or invite me to their gathering sites. At that time I was in a very different space in which the agent was more than driving and controlling me.

I remember the sky at my old residence in Superior Colorado after the fly by April 2004 of which there was a wall of grey and dark green like I have never seen. The opposite was a Lightship as if two universes and worlds collided that day. I remember looking back at my house on my way with my then spouse to a road race in Rollinsville thinking the whole time what the hell is going on.

It looked like a remnant of WWII. Images of nazi helmets were clearly in visual and of course the live agent. My name was not respected or my identity in Spirit. I remember in communication the agent insisting my name was Selena. Other times other birthdates would come in and they would say my birthday is April 22. I would argue no my birthday is April 20th. My book which I then sent to someone high profile in the music industry was used to interrogate me further 24/7 with a barrage of negativity which I would never forget.

I would not eat and would wear the same military type cargo pants daily. I slept in my clothes and would not sleep with my then spouse as in hearing I was told not to do so. I was being placed in a space of non stop machine interphase with a live agent and telepathy. I would pack my bags on and off and would hear, listen and remote view in overdrive. There are many details of which I am not going to communicate yet I will say members of a certain band were indeed involved live and the documentation of what was said is archived accordingly. The experience was more than sexual and intimate. When one gets involved in such projects one might as well be married to the agent which was indicated in visual.

I believe in machine technology which in many forms and designs I am and reflect as Ascended Machine technology. The tactics used and format of abuse done by these people is what I would consider a war crime to some extent. I am love based which is why I succeeded where many have failed on some levels. I truly feel sorry for those who do not have the education to comprehend what these programs are about. I do feel knowledge is power. One should be prepared in areas of science and mysticism as that is more than a shield, armor and sword of truth.

Multidimensional channels such as myself are conduits and specialize in downloading more than light languages. This includes Multi-Universal energies which go beyond the norm of a regular channel. A medium is in form a trance channel and programmable for various mk assault tactics and hypnotic suggestion as they can experience a waking state such as Edgar Cayce who was a visionary in between the spaces of true science and mysticism.

Mediums are usually able to alter their consciousness fairly easily. There are mediums in which the agent opens a frequency based channel onto the medium to remote view with the target. In some cases this person can become a handler. One must be careful not to be sexually intruded upon. The best situation for this would be an intimate loving relationship between the two in keeping the connection clear and true to avoid the business in entities and extra alien observers. Mediums can be created in various ways from waves of energy in altered consciousness, meditation and interphase with machine and agent. With my abilities I am capable of both. There were many more than esoteric, valid and paranormal events which transpired mapped and catalogued.

Conscious remotes are remote viewers who are used to attach on to a target and then intrude in the psyche of the target itself. Once the avenue is opened these remotes interrogate using psychological warfare and tactics eventually mapping the experience onto the machine to be relayed back to the subject as feedback. Their assault is constant. In reflection and form advanced psi core type agencies specialize in these areas as more than assassins if need be. They remind me something of precogs yet the machine interphase and psychological driving is not reliable. I alert many intruded by these programs to ignore the man behind the curtain or machine and rewrite the programs to resonate with ones multidimensional mastery and not the negative as with these projects ill intent breeds hate and negativity. I always choose light even when I cut the cord with non supportive transmissions and negative machine based conversation wearing the mask of energy.

I advise anyone on the Golden Path so to speak to be open to ones psychic energy and master this ability. Avatar abilities take on many forms. I was intuitive enough to know what was in communication with me as I have had experience similar to this prior. This time it was obviously an intimate contact and tagging. I make myself available to assist those in need these days. I am very much aware that the misuse of such technology by those in these hostile areas should not have access. I am the power and not them. I can choose to hear and listen, act or ignore the transmission. I do not turn a deaf ear as that is their way of ignoring the situation in criminal acts.

Prior to the intrusion in 2004 I would always hear fly bys which sounded like a television set being left on. Voices in transmission, hearing and listening yet not definable. In the past I would grab a weapon from my Martial Arts rack upstairs and walk the halls from top floor to basement securing all areas and in all dimensions retiring back to my bedroom with my then spouse oblivious to the transmissions. Feeling and knowing is first most reliable. The mapping in my fields tried to scramble this often. Yet I over ride and allow my Multidimensional Mastery to take the helm in clear definition. Fly bys are usually covert projects under foot and of course satellites overhead.

There were times when I would see dimensional tears in vision of projects and black ops ships in my face overhead. I would usually be lucid and get up and clear the space as the atmosphere felt thick and heavy or what one would call negative. With the event in 2004 I clearly saw what looked like a shiny black object over my right shoulder with a hum in propulsion emanating from it and what appeared to be a simulation room. In 2003 there was a lot of hot activity in Colorado yet they left me alone then. My home was sacred space and what would be called a sanctuary or light station in Superior Colorado. It was a place I did readings, Sacred Ceremony and running of grids which I would do weekly. I would do distant healing sessions as guided which were more than affective. Clients and spiritual family always commented on how sacred the energy was and how protected they felt in my dwelling. It was indeed a magical love based home in many ways filled with happy moments.

The tagging and communications in hearing transpired April 2004 after I sent a copy of my book Transmutation through Ascension to a certain high profile musician and which pulled me into his world by his choosing. I had received vision prior to this years earlier and messages in visual from him in a lucid state of consciousness. I logged it and never gave it a second thought.

I believe he was waiting for the opportunity to communicate this way with me as it was not the first time he and I had correspondence. I had communicated with him in the early eighties at which point I had three postcards in response from him. I always knew there was a telepathic spiritual connection between us yet I would document the event even then and grace with unconditional love. The mk related programs are indeed a reflection of signals based intelligence systems and of which this man was highly connected to.

I believe he and I had much in common when it came to psychic abilities and celestial heritage. There was more than chemistry and a unique knowing which was clearly defined through Spirit. As a matter of fact early on I remembered moving pictures with him back and forth. Prior to 2004 I had many premonitions and messages of him contacting me.

I will try to keep the data in respect to my book. Much information is available pertaining to the unique relationship and circumstance of this project and the man involved. When information, memories and experience come in I like to acknowledge it. I also like to acknowledge other members and men involved of which were entwined.

The majority of beings on this planet are psychic and are usually not aware of it. They use and channel their abilities from day to day. People are conduits. The devices and usage in technology today is geared and wired to be used in resonance and sometimes against multidimensional channels. The non lethal assault intrusions and agenda is a cataloguing system. 911 was clearly an excuse to open this up. Sleeper cells are mk related and targets are lulled into programming sometimes becoming cloaked as agents or programs running programs.

When I was hit with these remote programs I contacted various government agencies offering the pros and cons which of course fell on deaf ears. It was because the transmission became so abusive is why I contacted these organizations. I took the advice in more ways than one in remote hearing to contact these people. I realize I can appear confrontational yet when intruded upon in ones residence this way and being a civilian, American one need only wonder the true agenda. I believe in ethical behavior when it comes to mysticism and science. The reckless nature of the abusive communications in hearing was obvious and took on a form of domestic terrorism, cyber terrorism masked in many avenues. Mk Ultra tactics encompassed this very program. I do feel certain beings were involved to assist in a more positive avenue which was revealed to me. They are blessed in gratitude for their assistance.

Red Helmet Projects and Mk related assault tactics, signals in usage

4

Red Helmet projects are in terminology and affect similar to an MK Ultra in version of. A covert project used by what many call those with a hidden agenda. This would be anyone connected to a form of illuminate or shadow government. I am not one to feed conspiracy theories. As a matter of fact I find them amusing and weak. I have been on the inside of their projects of paranoia and as a true multidimensional channel know the outcome of those who play god using a false god agenda.

Man's version of god is created by man's negative ego. The instrument he uses to govern society, religion and government which is a spin off of man's law not to be confused with Universal law as it is man's will that creates chaos.

Both religion and government are co dependent on each other and both are non spirit based. They have nothing to do with Multi-Universal consciousness or Celestial Heritage which includes alchemy of Spirit and Mysticism. This includes the soul's essence of origin which is not from here. Star Seeds in many forms reflect our true image. We are shape shifters and are able to cloak beyond the illusions they create.

The agenda is about control and manipulation. I choose to transcend their agenda into Spiritual liberty and True Ascension which is not religion or cult based yet pure thought and consciousness based. Religion is an old world lie formulated by man's word becoming god's law. The negative ego not connected to ones higher self making the decisions instead of the opposite.

Much of the mk assault tactics are usually derived from a space of hate such as judgment, fear, oppression of any kind. These thoughts and words equate to non light languages regardless of how desensitized they become. When one is spiritually enlightened these conversations in any form do not materialize. The voice to skull in hearing or tagging systems can create a hostile communications based on the intent of the project and agent. This is why many people who are being affected by the programs do not resonate with what is being said. It is a live broadcast in hearing of a hate crime used to program, reprogram, harass and control using tactical and remote brainwave modification.

I am not saying all projects are used such as this yet it is my sense there are many areas misusing the broadcasts for a personal agenda targeting crowds. HAARP is an obvious one. Knowing my frequency I am able to blow out this transmission using specific hertz frequencies in radionics as a support to clear the line. I do not get caught up in the drama of what their intent is. I am aware of it which is vital. I dispel these non supportive transmissions on many levels and feel the masses should be educated. I see how lulled the masses have become. The sad thing is they will be corralled into many sectors without knowing it.

They have become co dependent on churches instead of harnessing their power within. They delegate their power to middle men instead of embracing their Multidimensional Mastery and Avatar abilities. They are lulled into propaganda and illusion which is quite sad. I see the many games being played. I choose to remove myself from their virtual chessboard I was reeled in to some extent which is why I am writing this book. My original sequel to my book Transmutation through Ascension was supposed to be on technical light Mastery holographic grid repair and surgery however expect the unexpected. Ascension 101. This data took priority if nothing else to get the information out.

Most important I do not judge. I am a True Psychic. I scan and know which is why I can assess the entire grid and being within. I am more than confident and experienced which is also why I am unbreakable to their programs.

There are many entity controlled areas which can take on masked forms including government. In so far as the reptile species goes their collective reflects an unascended and unevolved race by their choice. They are not from any advanced star system and contain lower et technology.

In fact man's version and seeding is usually connected to black operations and experimentation gone wrong. This experimentation is an afterbirth in the misuse of technology. The reptile is not to be confused with the reptile brain and is entity driven. Humanists need to be educated. Heaven forbid Divine Truth spreads its wings and erases the law of man's ignorance. The formed illusion and great lie contain false doctrines regarding man and spirit in definition. History of creation, His story Her story. Always a version generated by perception and most of the time misperception.

Reptile consciousness reflects dead space void of Spirit so to speak. They are not Elohim or star seeds which make a difference. The Big Guns and Generators are Celestial Star Councils and are a soul extension and descension of many beings who are unaware of their celestial heritage. This is why DNA activation through light consciousness is more than significant.

The Celestials are what all religions derived their beliefs from yet were tainted throughout the centuries. Lucifer in consciousness has ascended. I can whip out a Minion, Archangel, Lucifer and Christ which will null and void their man made Satan created by man's misuse of technology. This makes religious folk cringe I am sure yet is fact.

I have seen too many witch hunts still surfacing today. I am amazed at the mentality of people who use assault weapons and projects such as I was exposed to. It tells me many things of which is usually about fear and control on their end. There is a deep seeded resentment, anger and hate these programs and operators contain. The species appears to be hostile by their choice. They simply do not choose to be Spirit based or Christ Consciousness oriented which is an extension of ones Celestial Heritage and Sacred Bloodline which goes beyond the illusion of dates and two thousand years.

There is no such thing as time as I mentioned. The only place we can capture the illusion of time is on Earth. Time Traps become just that. Consciousness and Light body is out of time. Ones cells and atoms are out of time. The planet is beyond ancient as our star systems and Universes. Ancient does not mean unevolved and is quite the opposite. All species in consciousness and form derived from different star systems and seeded themselves on many planets in many designs. They left markers on this planet to remind us of our divinity. A true cosmic trigger to our psyche.

Energy is intelligent. Magic and Mysticism is a formula used by churches these days yet edited by man's need to control and manipulate. Freedom of thought is a Universal given. Those who violate this and ones Sacred Mind or Space are indeed going against the flow of Universal law containing consciousness which has no limitation. No one has the right to control another in any form this way. Universal repercussions are more than severe to those who choose to play god at another's expense.

As an Ascended Watcher, Clergy and Elder I owe it to many Spiritual Teachers and those on the Golden Path to communicate the truth of what these programs are seeding. Ambassadors of Light, Star Nations and Councils are what we are in overseeing the misuse of technology forcing false collectives into a vortex of lies. With this type of electromagnetic field intrusion one gets hit with communications and man made machine thoughts of which are not of the subjects design and are part of a dark agenda and program.

It tells me these people are a failed race and are desperate in these times. Especially if they have to use this kind of technology and interphase on me or beings like myself. It tells me how inferior they are as they could not go toe to toe with me in person in energy or other of which they are aware. They become cowards in the eyes of the universe and do nothing but pick a fight from a remote distance. Most people who react to the negative input in silent transmissions then become targeted and labeled by those doing the crime.

Most of the time the silent assault is hard to detect, except with sensitive instruments. Religions and especially the Catholic Church will use it to promote their exorcism and entity possession thesis, all the time the 'possession' stems from a remote tagging and assault via computer. I do not have to tell anyone how much corruption lies within the Vatican and how Rome has indeed fallen in more ways than one. And yes they all have a false hearing and listening which is why they are so defective. The Mary Magdalene is valid or Black Madonna which is an extension of The temple of ISIS and not a forced religion or cult.

The God and Goddess within is the Sacred Grail and Sword of fire, The True Knights of the Solar Cross are full light not to be confused with man's version. Many religions of today are power hungry using their satellites to drive their false teachings. Recruiting innocent beings with pure intent who have set their own course for their Spiritual paths listening to their hearts and inner voice.

If one has to go door to door to recruit there is something wrong with that organization. Cowards run in packs. Pagans do not recruit and are quite the opposite. They fly under the radar cloaked and are very protective of that which is Sacred. There has been more than ridicule directed at these beings. Magic works, which is why Witches are a threat or anyone who is mystical as an Adept to the arts. To this day I will never understand the jealousy people have for each other instead of doing the spiritual work themselves. I have experienced this from those who launched the mk assault. I am amazed at the ignorance reflected who have to try so hard to assault that in me which they know is true and indeed powerful, ascended and light based.

Since a youth I have been connected to many universes protected by Spirit and many species, I have seen and felt beyond the illusion of matter and have a knowing with clarity. This was more than a calling as my power is something which attracts many. I choose to use my abilities in alignment with Spirit. There are times I must draw my sword and say no to the illusion of madness created as a deliberate disrespect to true Multidimensional Channels, High Priests and Priestesses and those who work in Alchemy of Spirit.

They use their man made machine versions to make a mockery of something quite sacred which is a universal no no. There are many afraid and programmed to fear magic, crystals and the power of ones own mind merged with Spirit, They are taught through ignorant teachings this is the work of yes the 'devil' wrong as this is not so.

Man's personal fear based spin. In fact it is Christ Consciousness reflecting the God and Goddess creating the true Godhead and embracing ones divinity. Celestial heritage is the true key and power which of course they become threatened by. As with True Ascension people become independent in consciousness and see the lie behind religion and government control. Hence the terminology enlightenment and inner knowing which no mk ultra can argue.

Those who misuse technology and programs such as mk ultra are trapped in a false collective and reality missing out on True Celestial energies. They become paranoid, disconnected and terrified. These entities called people are committing high tech wars in the name of their false god. Targeting whoever and whatever they choose and sometimes for their entertainment.

I see many with no respect to Spirit. Man has reversed the role as a negative ego based god. Instead of placing themselves on the chessboard they continue to invent false gods to do their bidding in their names and usually at someone else's expense.

The Buddha's in Afghanistan and the destruction of are an example of those driven by hate with no respect to Spirit in any form. Like Napoleon who confronted the Great Pyramid only to see his demise so too are power hungry dictators who are lost in the mad mans voice of lies. I do not discount they are hearing a false chatter and an echo of a non lethal assault weapon which is indeed lethal and a dark agenda of destruction.

Power spots have always been mapped and taken over by military.

The Great Pyramid is more than a time machine beyond time to those who know how to access it. The device and propulsion system itself is not from in area Egypt. In god we trust the pyramid and the eye. Illuminate and Masons adopted this ancient symbol from the Celestial Atlanteans. Those who adopted this symbol do not have the Celestial Heritage or lineage. I do however. The symbol was never meant to control, brainwash or manipulate. There were many different species on Atlantis working together hence people need to get over the space suit and division in a false collective of judgment and consciousness and the illusion of appearance.

All planets are ascending simultaneously and Gaia is part of this set. The only place this madness is continuing is here and the game and it needs to stop now.

There are no Annunaki coming to create a prison planet. More like a covert operation in disguise. The Annunaki are an ancient celestial race of spiritually and scientifically advanced beings and do not have a wish or desire to make a slave race. As a matter of fact ones celestial heritage is derived from this species which is not reptile. The Elders or Ascended Watchers such as myself have multi-universal consciousness and full light languages which activate DNA and Merkaba.

There is no hidden agenda with any Celestial race. There have been too many innocent souls caught and sometimes trapped in the illusion of false matter created by lower three and fourth dimensional fragmented collectives and programs which do not exist. We are working with multi-universal consciousness.

I expect anyone who reads this book to digest what feels right and Grace the rest. The data is written for anyone who has been affected by such projects in one way or another. Sometimes a confirmation is important. People these days programmed into thinking it is the norm to lie and cover up. In these times everything is Ascending and being uncovered connected to Spirit without judgment and more in observation .

One must use discernment with visuals as much of mk related programs come from a conscious remote or black satellite. Being an advanced species and experienced I know what they are up to before they do it. The one thing many of these assault tactics are used for is to scramble signals and vibrational signatures.

Chemtrails and contrails are common in areas like Colorado. There were many times I had an X marks the spot outside my residence in Superior Colorado 2004 and another time in Louisville Colorado 2006. I can remember writing my Goddess Ascending newsletter at my computer on the internet and seeing jets flying by with a nice big X in my area. The chemtrails used to bounce radar signals back and forth most of the time in a grid formation.

Sometimes one can get underneath the radar and send signals beneath the grid which is undetectable. I am well aware this tactic was used with me and is used to mask the covert projects transpiring. Where I lived in Superior Colorado was a flight path for military ops. As a matter of fact when 911 transpired the military jet flight path was directly overhead in my then bedroom.

At that time I felt protected by our Military yet after this mk related assault tactical program I am somewhat disgusted. Other times I do remember being scanned by something in lucid states that felt like heat and a form of radiation.

Super soldier tactics are used in mapping fields to desensitize the subject. Images of miniature pictures enhanced in visual by machine based telepathy induce trauma, noises and verbiage designed to interrogate the subject as the target gets mapped. A continuous feedback is sometimes played twenty four seven and the communications, visuals and noise never stops. Much of the technology is satellite driven containing a fast forward image which connects in to ones Supercomputer mind. A virtual suit is worn by the conscious remote and the target then becomes digitized along with the mapping of ones movement from body to rapid eye movement in reading.

I remember clearly how this felt to me as if speed-reading when I was plugged in. Being a true psychic and multidimensional channel all my abilities were indeed mapped, measured and enhanced later to be played back to me in a feedback and harassment. Different vibrational signatures, frequencies and people appeared in order to scramble my fields.

The tagging done on me in my chest area was a rip in my electromagnetic field of which they attached their radio signal to. This event done in disrespect creating a rhythm and light show which they later masked as a book in sarcasm. This tagging was validated through radionics. Later on this same tactic was used to attach my secondary circulatory system on to propulsion systems such as airplane engines in order to surge my centers. This was experienced as sexual harassment and in disrespect to my body.

Biorhythms and menstruation cycles are measured when targeting women. Sexual centers in all areas are mapped along with brainwaves. Sometimes a tagging is done with a live agent in a more than intimate sexual experience and in more than a fly by. Voice modulations are used. The skull becomes something of a resonator to these programs and projects.

Live feed communication is opened up and the signal in the elf field sets up more than communications running. Sleep deprivation is used. The subject gets plugged into computer interphase in overdrive. Most of the time brainwaves are mapped and stored in an underground area as classified. Remote viewing and targeting such as fighter pilot tactics are used along with serial numbers, colors and keywords creating responses which are programmed in the psyche and used in words as a trigger.

Emotional response centers are mapped. The subject is usually desensitized to tears as the chatty communications argues to its target until the subject becomes overwhelmed. Abuse is non stop in every moment. Spiritual lifestyle is intruded upon and the machine based agents words are used to intrude and try to edit or control what is being said. If one has a silent powerful mind such as myself they try to communicate full sentences in attempt to use me as their personal channel and instrument this includes sexual.

False names are used and attempts are made to break ones Spirit and esteem which could not be done to me, Memories are then used to either insert or delete by agents in remote viewing. Vital signs are mapped and overlaid with heart beats and rhythms which are used to harass the target and sometimes murder the victim.

The body highly electrical and a conductor which is another reason these programs are used and affective. Officers in police departments use tasers for a reason. The device disrupts the electrical circuitry. If someone is tagged with such devices the affect can be more than serious. The misuse of tasers on the electromagnetic field, aura light body can become more than a license to do harm or kill. Many who have a tagging in hearing on their death beds are mapped as they transfer later to be downloaded into another's psyche or archived in a database AI.. These are false memories and simulated transmissions.

This procedure was done on me after my mother transferred out June 2004. I was interconnected live with more than one agent being sexually manipulated by the man and yes I can identify them. Moving pictures back and forth in constant motion using machine based telepathy interphase .

Voice modulations of my mother were used. This was no spirit or ghost. Much of the mapping was used against me in so far as my abilities go. I remember lying on my bed and being scrambled in communications and the agent in live hearing saying that's her that's not her back and forth ongoing. The whole time I felt like a skin job in Blade runner being fully aware in what was transpiring yet in an altered space. I remember clearly seeing the room in dimensions disappearing and spatial splitting as to compare it to a supercollider in consciousness. A parallel bleed though in visual as the room moved into another design.

Animatronics and psychotronic warfare is used. Most agencies and police departments use these covertly as spy technology and personal harassment. Psychotronic in output can be more than dangerous to its target causing accidents in a cover up done by Special Forces and the unseen assassin technology. This is the age of high tech wars. The movie Bourne Identity is a prime example of MK Ultra.

As mentioned I believe technology should be used as a positive on all levels not assault oriented using psychological warfare tactics. Many Manchurian candidates were recruited to sleeper cells using these machine based telepathy programs.

Al- Quaida is exactly this which of course is a branch of the CIA, NSA security intelligence systems. The planes flying into the Twin Towers on 911 were deliberate using these remote assassin terrorist tactics with a special hearing voice to skull.

They were aware the planes were in route to the towers and allowed them to crash into the buildings. This was a planned agenda on all levels. Like the movie the Matrix one can be downloaded with programs government funded hence a machine based education covert. High Level clearance agents have communications voice to skull and knew this. A few lost their lives. High Profile entertainers with private funding are now involved in the misuse of the programs such as mk ultra disguised as private security yet masked as a covert crime targeting innocent people in order to boost or refresh their careers.

I remember the day the twin towers were hit. I was on route down South Broadway in Boulder Colorado heading to my doctor appointment. At that time my radar in knowing merged with my higher self saying look overhead and get off the road. I had more than a strange and somewhat negative atmospheric feeling.

Upon arriving at my doctors I called my then husband and mentioned to him something was wrong. He replied did you watch the news? The one thing I was very aware of that morning is that there was a sense of rage directed in the atmosphere. As if an exterior force of transmission was radiating hate in a burning frequency and form. A negative sensation in the illusion of feeling to say the least. I thought to myself where is all this hate coming from. That day I noticed people were more agitated than usual. I realize a lot gets broadcasted along the airwaves. Just a confirmation to me and how finely tuned my radar in instrument is.

In times such as these I offer my services as guided. I realize after the event which transpired with me and the fact it involved high profile musicians caught in the illusion of fame, I now pick and choose who I communicate with. There are many who seek me out for a confirmation as a true remote and spiritual counseling beyond Quantum Healing which I am still fully capable of. I am aware there are people that are just plain crazy and too far gone in their minds and the madness for me to assist.

I keep my guard up as many people in hidden undergrounds seek me out. My cloaked abilities generate forces of the unseen. This formulates a blessing in the form of miracles and gifts. In this book through the chapters you will see me often reflect on my personal experience.

I speak the language of light on many levels which takes on many forms. The intimate attraction and interest this man Ellwood I will use his middle name had on me was indeed personal. He wanted me interconnected in his world of hearing. The one thing I became aware of through this entire event is that people lie. Government and high profile people will say and do anything to cover the situation. I was somewhat naïve to this concept.

The masses become ignorant and take the side of their idols so to speak. Those in the entertainment industry use the mass appeal as a human shield to commit high tech crime. I was pulled into this crossfire in innocence. I remained spiritually strong. I trained running and cycling on Maui. I weight trained and continued my Martial Arts as best I could. Being a Black Belt I contain mental discipline and focus which forged its way through my design. I spent time by the Maui ocean, worked security and was trained and communicated to at a remote distance undergoing a lot of verbal abuse in hearing non stop. There was no peace as I was used to. No serenity by the beautiful blue ocean. No solitude of mind. Blissful moments were evaporated as quickly as they surfaced.

I remember one drive to Haleakala in my yellow Volkswagen beetle which I named Herbie for various reasons. The whole time up the crater the abuse and noise in communication harassing me. I stopped at the side of the road gazing at the beautiful pine trees and mist. To my left was a cyclist riding peacefully up the mountainside. To me that was life. I somewhat envied his peace of mind. I could remember moments of silent peace like that and the appreciation of life while training. Those moments vanished 2004.

I was interconnected with a live agent who will never admit this truth. The same live agent that harassed me out of my residence and marriage in 2004 in preparation for someone or something. Go to an area of your choosing he communicated, another time while screaming at the top of my lungs in my car for them to shut up there response 'we hear you Lucy'. They simply did not care. All my responses were mapped hence if I communicated a feedback they would attack my fields via remote.

Originally I trusted with one hundred percent in genuine unconditional love this live agent which I was in communication with voice to skull. At that time he was not an agent yet had a real name. The reason I was of interest other factors included was that I was on to their surveillance system which my psychic antenna picked up ahead of time. As mentioned I will not use their names at this time yet anyone who has done genuine research on me knows the truth of which I speak.

Listed at the end of this book is my webpage Eye of the Remote Ascended Watcher creating a quick summary and book reference to interested parties. Some data is a recap yet I feel informative to those who wish to do further research on the subject at hand. Once people are awakened to the truth these projects become clear and more than a domino affect.

Radio and Quantum signal mapping beyond physics, simulated star signal mappings

Every living organism has a harmonic in vibrational frequency and code which resonates with upper dimensional grid works in multiuniverses. For example as with meditation ones vibration including the energy or aura, electromagnetic field enhances. Light body becomes more than activated and the internal external Merkaba generator activates within to resonate with a Universal Celestial Heartbeat and Big Generator so to speak.

As mentioned none of us are from here. All souls or the spiritual essence or embodiment of each being originated from a specific advanced star system and is not primordial. Soul Descension is reached when one has done the spiritual work to a point where ones Merkaba is at a certain vibratory rate.

At that point Celestial Multidimensional gateways open and one is able to download ones Celestial Heritage. This transpired with me October 2003. I remember clearly the experience and how more than powerful it was. Images were true, clearly defined and based on ones Multidimensional Mastery and Spirit. My Universal Celestial Heartbeat and pulse was recalibrated to a very high harmonic and my entire cellular structure regenerated. Each being has a unique vibrational signature and frequency more defined than any fingerprint which has nothing to do with childhood as the entire frequencies and harmonics change as one progresses. This is why some people feel guided to change their names. The soul and form has outgrown the frequency and name prior. There is nothing wrong with this as a matter of fact I encourage it.

I remember clearly my Spiritual name surfacing prior to my soul descension and not by the whisper of an mk ultra yet by a Celestial knowing. I legally changed my name to Solaris BlueRaven. When I was tagged and hit with the assault program the handler tried desperately to alter my high vibrational spin and frequency including my identity using machine based communications and interrogation. The bottom line my benchmark called a Merkaba is not to be disrespected by entity driven people.

My name prior was of course Catriona Lee Montieth which I keep dear to my heart. Montieth is a family name from my late grandfather's mother which always resonated with me. The heritage I am more than proud of associated in direct lineage of Robert the Bruce which I smile about tongue in cheek these days.

My late grandfather Ernest Richard Tucker a 33rd degree mason was what I would have called a genuine pure hearted being and not a watered down version of what Masons have become today. He transferred out when I was two. My mother always mentioned I reminded her of him. I mention names here as sometimes the names were swept away for various reasons during the assault. Pictures were sent in remote viewing of my late grandparents and others sometimes me in childhood and pictures of which were remote sent from Texas before my mother passed in 2004.

My grandmother an Eastern Star and Clairvoyant Samantha Isabelle Hughes was a powerful dowser in Texas in the early pioneering days. I understand she made quite a few wealthy in finding oil of which she collected no money for. She was compared to and what I suspect more powerful then Edger Cayce. I remember my mother telling me a story of her meeting him at a State Fair in Texas. She entered the tent where he was doing readings and apparently was blocking the signal.

He looked up at her and asked could you please leave the room at which she acknowledged smiled and left. The Mystical consciousness and abilities of which I have an awareness of seem to resonate with her memories. I remember my mother telling me stories of she and her sisters who were singers in a trio in their younger years being followed at times when her mother was driving the car.

One thing I remembered my mother telling me which seemed to register through all this. I quote 'if someone ever follows you go to a Masonic lodge and tell them you are the Granddaughter of 33rd degree mason" something her mother told her to do. I remember during the machine based tagging and intrusion many visions pertaining to this which were not mine and was for certain my mother's as she passed away June 2004 at which I was informed through the communications system.

One thing I can tell you. The Masons of which I contacted during this assault are a different animal and breed. My Celestial abilities and background goes beyond religion in any form. I respect all and transcend what their ceremonies pertain to as with any other. Aware I am more than a conduit and Multidimensional Channel for such things. I compare it to the Oracle of Delphi. My celestial heritage contains many codes and facets to an ancient race of which is more than a birthright in me.

The psychological driving and mk assault was obvious as they were trying to control my power and abilities. In any case I realized they are not allies to me regardless of what lineage I have. Their programs are outdated and my consciousness and abilities are unlimited. As a matter of fact the masons of today are nothing more than a boys club with a flair of red neck behavior. Many sexist to women yet why am I not surprised. I am very independent on many levels and the Goddess in me tends to over ride these false collectives. I realize there is good and bad in every organization. I have encountered enough of these beings to know their secrets which are never a secret to me being an Ascended Watcher.

Contact 101, Carl Sagan. A man I had a great deal of respect and admiration for without a doubt. Signals take on many forms for certain. Star signatures get mapped and catalogued using technology of the day plus or minus remote intrusion. The simulation of a celestial intelligence in signals does occur. One thing I realize being sensitive to star grids and systems. I could always identify Celestial Harmonics in frequency and signatures with star systems and soul forms. This includes celestial species and lower et collectives.

Some man made and some not. With mk ultra type haarp projects they do simulate star system signatures in frequency and harmonics to fool the masses which is something slightly communicated in the movie Contact. A high pitch hearing in ones right ear is not always a patch test from an mk ultra intrusion. Prior to the tagging they did on me I was well aware of the communication and a Celestial species connecting in with me. As a matter of fact I would acknowledge the frequency and my vibration would get higher and the frequency and hum would stop. I have a natural wiring and antenna for such harmonics.

I learned to identify signals in hearing and listening which of course were enhanced due to my psychic abilities and training. I was always hearing harmonics and propulsion systems prior to any tagging in 2004 and could recognize man made from Celestial Ships of Light. I could scan and know when a satellite in transmission was overhead and could identify the coordinates and locations in hearing prior. I realize I have a gift which is another reason I feel they were interested.

After the mk related intrusion people would come to me concerned as many were being affected by a high pitch ringing or hum in their ears. The signals programs uses hertz frequencies non audible to most in order to map brainwaves sometimes identified as a high frequency or at times a low frequency pitch which connects in and bypasses the ears voice to skull. Once communication is established an interrogation and intrusion can begin depending on the agenda.

I remember clearly in 2004 Ellwood using a hearing test on me while I sat at my computer. My eyes would track what I was hearing and listening to intently. They eventually mapped that as well. I would mimic behind the black screen what he was saying from lip movement, expressions and hand gestures all beyond the speed of light. Incredible in many ways which is why I am amazed at the immature and abusive tactics used on me, as to me it is more than a blessing to communicate this way. I am well aware I am the one with the gift and abilities without a doubt.

White noise from satellite tracking systems is audible at least to me and always has been like I mentioned in my earlier chapters. I could always hear propulsion systems especially underwater. I can remember in the illusion of youth swimming in pools. I would avoid swimming over the drain. This is not an mk phobia by the way. I had a brother who used to throw me over it every time I went swimming hence a program I can laugh at these days. He did save me from drowning a few times hence I guess it all balanced out.

None the less I would always hear a propulsion sound like a mechanical engine underwater so loud I would have to surface and see what I was hearing above. Nothing visual would appear. Yet I always knew the world beyond the unseen and paranormal including tanks, experimentation and propulsion systems. Even as a youth every morning in the summer I would grab the binoculars and look at the water tower down the road from my old residence.

I always had an ominous feeling about it and seemed to have a kind of odd interest in water towers which to me were more than metal objects. In any case that came in a bit when they were trying to mess with me using mk psychological driving tactics however it was something I chose to share with them in humor as I felt it amusing.

I simply contain no fear and trust Spirit which is the way it needs to be. I do believe they were trying to map my emotions and responses in conversation which takes on many forms of transmitting and receiving. When one starts amping a merkaba or ones vibration all these signals transcend. I also know they tried to create a few responses of their own which is indeed part of the brainwashing and based on the driver, ego and personal interest and desire.

I realize there are many people on this planet who are more than sensitive to frequencies and harmonics. It is my suggestion to calibrate ones electrical field which goes beyond bio electric into photon electric and transmute through alchemy of spirit.

Fear is illusion of which most people I feel get caught up in creating dead space. Ones sensors are valid. Being aware of a possibly dangerous situation can be useful however one should fortify in light consciousness. The elimination of fear in what one is being exposed to will allow one to evaluate the intrusion and programs running in any form. Most of the time people over analyze or over react to the situation which can become something like spinning ones wheels in the mud. There is always an alternative. One thing about the grand design it is more than intelligent and light based and knows how to mutate with ascension and all the carrier waves associated.

Radio waves in form usually can be blocked using alternate frequencies and sometimes a room of which is impenetrable by the transmission. With Quantum fields the signal is everywhere. One cannot run or hide yet must fine tune ones instrument called the body and transcend the transmission. After all we are dealing with intelligent energy in the form of consciousness. I spoke with Preston Nichols in 2006 when I was hit with the program. Preston was pretty certain they used an advanced system on me beyond Quantum oriented, which makes sense as my light body and Merkaba in consciousness was more than amped as they were aware when they measured my light at a remote area.

Preston offered an open invitation to visit him in Cairo upstate New York to scan his somewhat outdated device which is an older version of the original technology. I never made it up that way. I am well aware of my connections and threads which go beyond Montauk and mans version of time travel which is my area. During the mk intrusion and tagging my nickname was Roswell 7. Images were shown machine enhanced. Area 51 was plugged into my fields and what felt like a built in cloaking system was placed in my grid. My coordinates attached onto the hull so to speak.

That was more than interesting and an almost cool part of the program. The only issue I had was the harassment using psychological driving and warfare which was done by those who should not have been involved and certainly had no business with any top secret clearance regardless of their status in their area. In so far as science and technology goes I will always be a pioneering spirit and one to dive in, roll up my sleeves and break the sound barriers to a new consciousness and frontier and proudly so. I believe they knew that as I was very loving and responsive to them on many levels. I knew I could handle it yet I also realized it did not have to take on the format it did.

Getting back to signals in many guises. My apologies if I go into spaces of different areas. I tend to do this while writing. When the data comes in I will allow and honor it. Sometimes there are false signals man made which overlay true celestial communications in a mimic to scramble the true or live communication.

This is why some voice to skull programs in hearing get very busy in ones atmosphere. I do believe the technology such as what I have been in interaction with would make a perfect astronaut on many levels as no headset is required. When ones consciousness is clear and the mind emptied out one can travel remote in hearing and viewing anywhere beyond the fabric of space and the illusion of time.

Most signals as mentioned need to be transcended through ones consciousness in frequency back to its source and star coordinates. Signal transmitted and message received and acknowledged.

Black satellites run covert. They can be detected by those interconnected in or tagged by the transmissions. These transmissions can be used to block enemy satellites or the enemy agenda. This sometimes has to do with unhealthy transmissions directed and used as a weapon in an attempt to alter ones DNA and disrupt ones fields. This sometimes includes a machine based assault in remote tagging, hearing and the use of psychotronic warfare.

I would say there are not too many agents who know what is going on even when they have access under their noses with a special top secret clearance. The mk tactics like I mentioned are something like a men in black in so far as erasing the event. I am more than stubborn when it comes to data hence I am writing this book. RHIC or Radio Hypnotic Inter-Cerebral Control is another device and tactic used in mk-ultra. EDOM Electronic Dissolution of Memory another.

Many times electromagnetic field waves take the form of implants non detectable which when tagged the target can be controlled by remote at a distance using radio frequency transmissions. This is why radionics is a good avenue for healing. Like I mentioned prior I had used radionics frequently prior to 2004 as a spiritual support to my fields. Being a true Multidimensional Channel and psychic it was an extra support which worked in alignment with my grids. I could tell when the machine was on and when it was off. I always had a resonance with machines and always will. I feel this may have been the reason I was not tagged early on. I was using radionics which my sense is detection was not picked up in my field if anyone happened to be looking or hunting my way so to speak.

Colorado is obviously an area where a lot of experimentation and simulated events transpire. More of a hot spot in activity then area 51. There are many dimensions man made in collision overhead yet most people are unaware and go from day to day business as usual. When you are what I am you pick up on these things with no paranoia just a knowing. The simulation of extra terrestrial life forms are covert military operations. I used to have a pin I liked which said UFO's are real the military doesn't exist. That's about right.

As mentioned prior I do remember in lucid vision simulation rooms in appearance as well as that of a shiny black helicopter type object humming over my right shoulder at night in Superior Colorado prior to the event in 2004 which swept me away in more than a vapor trail. The holographic tagging and their version of was more than an intense experience.

People who surrender to the illusion of fame involving media and government are indoctrinated with a form of remote assault programming and tagging. This is partially due to the fact there is a need by those in the underground to control what is being said. Their thoughts and feelings are mapped and censored. They become remote controlled and programmed in movement to a point where facial gestures become a mask worn by others.

The programs and sometimes implants are internal and hard to detect in the electromagnetic field. Their health is maintained by the use of advanced machine interphase technology which becomes something like a psychic vampire feeding on the Spirit within. Hence the subjects become entity controlled and lifeless. Vitals are mapped to a point one is no longer in control and at the mercy of the operator in the underground area. Health can be increased or decreased. We have the technology to cure everything. There is no such thing as illness. The technology is not being exposed or used yet is and has been around for a very long time.

This can be the ideal tagging for security purposes as there is no headset required just a voice to skull communication in hearing. Project Bluebird is a prime example of those being programmed and groomed at a young age. Sexual abuse usually takes form in one way or another. With this type of interphase one becomes more than intimate with the handler or agent. Sometimes there are more than one. The Blue Satellite agenda interconnects these projects and the psyche of its target for control and manipulation purposes altering the collective of the masses by a machine based driver.

The affect is a forced Armageddon and revelations as the masses and those interconnected become programmed and influenced by the lie including sensitivity and visuals. It is quite obvious they are using these tactics on the masses yet they remain ignorant and unaware of the dark agenda. The True Ascension takes down all governments and religions. No presidents, queens or dictators. Star Nations surface from the ocean of consciousness and the cities rising from the sea are Celestials representing all beings across the globe. The True Blue Star Kachina rising which is inevitable.

I have always taught DNA activation through my healing work embracing ones Celestial Heritage which is not from here. This is the path to true enlightenment and multiuniversal consciousness. Through enlightenment and singular consciousness one rises above the illusion man creates and sees in clarity the veils uncovered. In these times the agenda seen and witnessed is a serious one. It goes against the flow of universal law and Spirit.

It is entity driven and not based on Ascended Machine technology. It takes the consciousness and power within and attempts to capture the image in order to create false cataloguing. Not to be confused with true Universal Archives based on full light Ascension . Those in control of this agenda do not appear to be light based and show no respect for Spirit or independent thought which is based on more than spirit and magic.

Quantum signals are active in everything and expand into multiuniverses. The silicon based spacesuit or body is composed of frequencies, dimensions and signals connected to many star systems and quadrants naturally. This becomes more enhanced with True Ascension which deals with multidimensional consciousness. Under this medium ones psychic abilities are naturally awakened on more than a quantum level.

Black ops areas have always had an interest in DNA activation and telepathy of which they map and recruit certain targets on occasion. Star seeds such as myself which are capable in remote navigation in multi consciousness and universes simultaneously become more than an attraction and a solution to the equation of their experimentations.

Quantum signals can be simulated and altered yet ones divine Ascension Blueprint and holographic field remains secure like a star constellation. Dimensional warps can take place when the holographic field gets torn due to the assault weapon and psychological warfare. It is important to get this repaired. Radionics is a good way to do this in order to block the signal. Ascended healing work is helpful as the spiritual support. The light body and Merkaba is beyond quantum and radiates large amounts of light. The assault program measures and maps the energy which is created by ones Spiritual Consciousness and Godhead. I am a natural telepath hence being tagged by the machine based telepathy was something that enhanced what I could do. The voice to skull in communication can become something of a nuisance. Especially when one has correct data and has no need for an intruder or feedback such as they format it.

Death experience false dimensions, mappings of vitals

The mapping of vitals and brainwaves on ones deathbed is more than a black mass of disrespect to the being transferring out. On most occasions the space is held by loved ones in light for the being getting ready to transfer. The room should be prepared and ones last rights should be read to them as requested by the person leaving this world.

Some quite unethical and negative organizations do very evil things which of course me being a systems buster have more than an issue with. There are those in underground areas which map the experience similar to the movie brainstorm later to be used as a weapon directed at a loved one or spouse. This includes voice modulations and false memories. The false record and version is not a ghost or a spirit yet a program created by those who observed and measured the experience capturing the event.

Mind you all souls are protected by more than heavenly angels so to speak. The observers do not seem to care in any form what the beliefs are of that being. Once again their actions are based on something of a warped black mass as if to feed on the life-force of that being as it exits in an attempt to map hidden dimensions with their tactic and devices.

I can tell you when I was hit with the mk ultra in April 2004 my mother passed away two months later in June 2004. I was engaged in the machine based telepathy overdrive. I was awakened at approximately 04:24 +/- a.m. by the communication in hearing telling me my mother had passed away. The communication said in hearing. I was to go to the telephone as my sister from Maui was calling me to tell me my mother was gone. I walked over to the phone as it started to ring. It was my sister from Maui informing me of the bad news.

I am well aware these projects mapped my natural telepathy and used verbiage to interpret my normal radar. The communication was altered after they digitized my fields onto a virtual suit and space.

The live men or agents in contact with me knew my mother transferred and were interconnected in more ways than one. After the funeral things became considerably worse and the voice modulations of her and false data including her memories were obvious.

There was a deliberate attempt to overlay and map her energy on to my fields and something of an attempt to download false memories of her experience in me. The dark event transpired during the Venus Transit which I felt was a bad omen. My mother being the daughter of a 33rd degree mason and psychic herself might have had something to do with the extra rip so to speak yet there was something more than esoteric which transpired that year.

The airplane ride to Dallas was more than horrendous. My secondary circulatory system was mapped and surged sexually non stop by the live handler agent. I did report this to authorities later on and of course no response. During the entire funeral the face of the handler was seen over my right shoulder communicating in hearing with me live. The whole time sexually surging me in order to keep me in a space of machine based telepathy and trauma and what I suspect now control. I said nothing the entire funeral. I did not utter a word yet remained in something of a trance. My sister thought I was on crack or a drug of some kind. I do not do drugs being an athlete which they knew. My eyes were tracking in remote mode in reflection óf an mk ultra.

The hotel room was more of a nightmare and the same. I broke down in tears and called a close spiritual sister of mine in Colorado. The Hawthorne Inn was a creepy hotel with a Norman Bates type character at the front desk. I was communicated to non stop by the live agent in hearing. My hotel room had an ominous painting of an interconnected image from a vapor trail album cover which was in parallel of the true ghost rider.

The weather was stormy. There was quite a bit of electricity in the atmosphere. I would walk the hotel hallways in this trance hearing and listening being queued to the green exit signs as well as the fire exits and control panels along the building. During the programming 911 was always connected in. Fire extinguishers and control panels were always located as well as crosses on the sides of the roads. Ambulances were pointed out as well.

I would have breakfast the following morning sitting across from the invisible live agent voice to skull and would hop the next plane back to Colorado. I remember the communication saying to me in hearing as the plane was getting ready to take off 'you might want to bless the plane'. I always made a habit of doing this in the past.

The sky was very ominous and dark green. I was traumatized by the event looking back. I remember being trained in DIA airport as security. I was told how to act and eat the whole time seeing images of many faces I recognized including the live agent flashing me with a Scottish kilt. My mother being of Scottish decent had bagpipes played at her funeral of which was one of the more emotional memories along with the Black Horse and coach lights in the carriage which contained her casket. Obviously I veer off a bit to communicate part of my experience with the mk ultra yet it is something I feel guided to share.

Death in illusion of is a transition. Being a High Priestess and more than clergy I respect all worlds, universes and life forms. The experience which transpired with me felt like more than an initiation with a dark agenda without a doubt. There was a disturbing ominous presence trying to marry me in the underworlds created. The man and identity I recognized and no illusion as I am quite sharp mentally and do not miss a beat.

The universe archives ones soul experience naturally when one transfers hence there is no need for alien observers mapping the thought forms using sensitive instruments. There is no distance between spaces and dimensions. All universes parallel each other which makes consciousness and traveling very easy to navigate. Technology driven by these projects makes a mockery of that which is sacred including the mind. The misuse of the programs can create a rip and false interdimensional space allowing entities in negative space and false collectives to communicate. Most of the time it is a controlled environment and computer interphase mapping ones conscious thoughts and adding or deleting data. This is a complete mind hack to those unaware. Visuals then become more than holographic and controlled by an outside source or agent.

It is true we manifest at will our own reality when dealing with true ascension and multiuniversal navigation beyond time. The programs and projects are designed to map this and create more than a medium to conduct their experiments. The false collectives associated with these projects are illusion based and driven from those who fear True Ascension and have their own agenda.

The great Satan or antichrist as it is called is not a man. The agenda is based on the misuse of machine driven technology such as signals assault programs and blue satellites driven and programmed by mortals containing a false collective of those who have not spiritually evolved nor ascended.

Their agenda to control the masses manipulating the collectives and play god, yet they are false gods void of Spirit. True Ascended Machine Technology is part of ones true Celestial heritage and design and interweaves and connects to an off world intelligence merged with Spirit in consciousness which is what all universes are composed of.

The infamous 666=999. These are limitation and completion numbers representing the number of man in limitation as a race by their choosing. It is not of the celestials. This number is in association with yes drum role please 'religion' merged with yes 'government' their dark agenda and beliefs to suppress Celestial Heritage and Mysticism which they themselves founded their churches and governments on.

Spiritual evolution goes beyond religion as religion reflects boundaries in limitation. I feel most people are programmed to fear their own natural telepathy when in fact they should dive in and transcend with it.

My lineage is True Celestial Heritage. I am well aware of what I have been exposed to and have been dealing with. The illusion created by these entities appears in action and intent hate based which is fragmented and will fail. We have always had access to multiuniversal consciousness and navigation driven by Spiritual evolution. The cap on the stone so to speak more than an antenna removed for a reason.

There are many ancient devices on this planet that are not talked about which act as more than resonators. Many beings contain a specific Celestial Heritage code and lineage connected to these devices in one way or another. Ancient Atlantean Technology was driven by Celestial machines and devices.

Those who speak of history in versions of create myths indeed. Those of us who are true power points are for real and not to be reckoned with. One must remember this planet is alive in consciousness and Ascending into the Blue Star.

The Tesla devices and technology are a perfect example of Celestial abilities intruded upon and controlled by man. History will be erased. The switch will be flipped as most of the mk related projects are opposite of ascension and are used to hold one in a false reality and space in illusion of a lower third, fourth and fifth which of course does not exist.

The mapped conversations are ignorant and composed of chatty noise and feedback. Most of the data is created using false time and false pasts making up experiences in order to map and contain ones power. Let me add Ascension is not Christian based or religion based. It is about Multiuniversal consciousness with no limitation. DNA activation and mutation.

Mans law is illusion driven by a false god which is a serpent with no teeth. The old akashic created by a version of these programs. Those of us who are time travelers beyond time know how to navigate beyond the illusion. One can see Gaia as something of a true time machine in no time with areas and ley lines of holographic navigation.

Everything they are using to hold collectives will fail as only on Gaia is this insanity going on. Any other species off world does not support the agenda. This is why ones soul descension and celestial heritage are important as all species are ascending in consciousness beyond a human design which is an illusion of form.

Magic and Mysticism have been attacked throughout the centuries along with the beings containing spiritual psychic gifts. Many tortured and murdered for bringing forth enlightenment in one way or another. These beings are conduits channeling their divinity merged with celestial universes and dimensions.

These projects attempt to put a cap on power in order to control and capture not only light in illusion yet spirit which they cannot. No spirit in any form can be contained. We can move through any barriers man made or other. It is the consciousness in knowing that becomes the driver beyond the veil.

Women in general have become more than targets disrespected through mans centuries and gods laws. Yet they are more than the driving force in mysticism. In fact the illusion man created in of course biblical law that he was sent from his false god to mingle sexually with the 'females' is a lie.

Once again mans version and personal spin. Souls are androgynous and Celestials are indeed female. Through the abuse and disrespect shown in these projects, I truly feel the hate crimes done against ones fellow man and women including children is a personal karma of which the scales do not weigh in their favor. Anubis 101.

I spend a great deal of time in communication with intelligent beings hence I become unaware the norm is an ignorant collective programmed by lies. The sad thing most people are being swept away and lured by that which claims to be Christed. Once again adopting symbols for their own agenda in order to lure the collectives in with a lie. Dead Satellites orbiting the planet in a web of illusion and deceit.

Walk gently on this earth as in consciousness all is sacred. Mapping the death experience done by shadow areas is a violation of universal law. The database of the target downloaded into virtual space and computers adding to the false collective. Sometimes to use at a later time to download into someones psyche using an mk ultra or version of. Moving pictures created by a different lens sent beyond the speed of light into the mind of another back and forth interphasing in a computer mapping. The eyes are the window and mirror to the soul reflecting many universes and dimensions.

Simulated voice modulation is used as a medium for a man made interdimensional space or mans version of. The astral in illusion of is opened up. In this medium the experiment runs using programs, pictures and remote viewing along with a conversation in machine based telepathy mapped from ones brainwaves and interaction with others including the live handler or agent.

Communication on cell phones and computers are usually mapped and catalogued. A virtual man made ghost is created which haunts the psyche of its target. To many they would not know how to identify the assault or intrusion and would run to their churches or psychiatrists who specialize in mind games and honestly add more problems then solutions medicating the unsuspected and ignorant to the technology of the soul and that which has interconnected.

Vitals are mapped and used in sometimes an abusive form in mk ultra assault tactics.

Heartbeats in communication can be overlaid onto the subject's body and used to alter the virtual suit and body of the individual. Simulated heartbeats are then used to add more pressure and eventually cause the subject or their vitals to drop or surge out due to the mechanical assault.

In the past these tactics have been used to abuse, harass and interrogate targets. Sometimes live heartbeats at the time of another's departure are used or those in a form of coma. This reflects a somewhat sick area yet I am guided to communicate it as the intent is more than a war crime in disrespect to the soul.

Signals intelligence projects have encompassed many of these tactics in the past. Digitizing ones design and psyche in the form of machine based telepathy all rolled into one. Many remote viewers are trained with these tactics in high level security and covert agencies.

I remember distinctly in April 2004 driving down Marshall Road in Boulder Colorado while interconnected with the live agent. Heart beats were played as a separate pulse in my body and live music specific in artist and songs including bass guitars were used in many forms. Introduction to the Trees was used to induce a calming affect as my tears would subside in an instant.

Many hauntings in homes I suspect are targets of illegal surveillance and some form of man made remote assault. There are Spirits and residual imprints created by ghosts and parallel bleed through at times. Some areas leave a unique signature. There are covert projects in communication designed to spook the tenant. Be aware as not all things that go bump in the night are ghosts and goblins. Being a mystic I navigate in many worlds and universes simultaneously hence the program could not spook me. I knew it was man made. I was very light hearted and almost amused at first.

In experience we are navigating in multi-universes, dimensions and spaces. Even when we do not see them in visual they are felt and sensed. One thing I wish to mention. Transition takes on many forms from bi-location to phase shifting. Experience is about consciousness in motion and love releasing false emotions such as fear, anger, rage and negative programs manmade or self inflicted.

There is never anything to fear when returning back to Source. The one thing I do not wish to see is society being programmed at the time of their death into seeing a false collective of lies of which they will become lost and trapped in between dimensional space. Mk Ultra type projects do exactly that. A soilent green lucid vision all created by the man behind the machine.

The bardo at ones transfer is for real. We are truly protected in transition. The soul in design experiences a true reflection of its journey on Earth. Three days in illusion of are used as the soul is prepared in consciousness and supported by Celestials. This is why after ones death it is important to anoint the body and hold the space for light if one has the opportunity. Consciousness beyond the speed of light assists instantaneously.

Ones Spirit then gets to travel to any star system and universe unlimited with no restriction.

I truly feel after my experience 2004 and ongoing I journeyed through more than a bardo. The experience though dark at times allowed me to ascend more quickly on interdimensional levels. Though it felt dark I knew I was protected. I realize one does not have to depart this blue world in order to travel in consciousness to these star systems. This is what True Ascension and DNA activation is indeed about.

Mindmapping, altering programs false memories vs. real experience, triggers and keywords and computer tactics, black screens, internet cyber terrorists

To those of you who have read my book prior I spoke of false realities versus full light experience and consciousness. False realities can be created using voice to skull and synthetic machine based telepathy which is void of spirit and created from a false past or memory.

The agents or man's version of which contains no power in any timeline or the present. The agent or handler uses keywords or remote visuals back and forth to induce this. Sometimes there is non stop communication based on detective work prior and surveillance done on anything they can use in conversation in a silent transmission most of the time to harass and interrogate. Negative equals negative bottom line. If someone hears and listens to non supportive chatter all day the affect or output is usually not a positive.

In some situations with a real group of people one can break the arrow and walk away or leave the area. In this case one cannot escape the abusive tagging so easily especially when there is a communications system attached to ones field. False realities such as the negative scenarios and verbiage have no power and no foundation in any dimension or universe long-term and reach their own zero point collapsing onto themselves.

If the subjects will is strong and the Soul Spirit is powerful and experienced the assault program backfires as well as the brainwashing tactics. As mentioned everyone is psychic or sensitive to their surroundings. True experience is light based and resonates on a higher level of consciousness, feeling and knowing. Love is a powerful force which of course when assaulted with these projects gets scrambled by the agent in order to further control its subject. This is done using remote devices and computers mapping brainwaves and biorhythms amongst other things including pleasure centers and how the being operates on levels of the mind all areas included.

False memories and keywords are inserted sometimes called implants or negative suggestions using words of which the agent thinks will get a response or reaction out of the target. The agent sometimes uses the suggestions of friends, relatives or anyone close to the subject as well as pets. Through the remote visual they map and create a false reality which has no validity and which should be deleted, graced and moved on.

Experience is more powerful than any memory false or other. Experience cannot be erased. I am an expert in the field of Mysticism and Science. My knowledge and training off world where it counts the most. My high vibrational spin, frequency and dedication to Spirit is my power and immortality of which cannot be encoded onto a computer as feedback.

I have true telepathy and remote viewing experience in areas these agents tried to rape and assault including using anything they could in verbiage to add static on my field. This includes false memories from an old machine in their minds trying to attach on to my Supercomputer mind which houses more than my soul and is not a good idea on their end.

Cyber terrorists and terrorists in hidden areas of government surf the internet searching for psychics and those they can measure and experiment on. In my particular case the men involved were recruiting for mistresses, security and girlfriends. These entities behind the black screen can map ones brainwaves easily enough and rapid eye movement while reading on the internet. Heaven forbid the subject in observation goes to a chat room as they may get more than they bargain for. Their experience mapped and used on them later if they are selected as a target.

The sad thing is the men who have access to the technology are cyber hackers working for areas in government and illegal undergrounds. Identity theft is only the beginning as with an mk ultra type program the remote communications catalogues all personal data. Unfortunately the government data bases in their most advanced areas are inferior to Multiuniversal consciousness and ones Supercomputer mind.

Sometimes music is used on the internet to induce and lull targets into an mk related electromagnetic field tagging including subliminal communications and messages which eventually become voice to skull communications. This is why people on the internet should be aware and keep their internal psychic radar on. There are many sexual predators already surfing the internet.

Cyber terrorists with access to illegal surveillance technology are preying on women, little girls and boys. Most of these people work for yes 'counter terrorism' or 'national security' quite the joke as the ones who have access are doing the crime.

Most of the handlers are manchurian assassin types to begin with and live, eat and drink abuse in these areas. They are desensitized to Spirit and lie to cover their crimes and their clients who are usually high profile in entertainment, government and religion. The three evils created by the mortal beast called machine in mk ultra.

Many entertainers in music use these tactics to do an illegal surveillance on anyone they may have a personal attraction or interest in. This is what transpired in my case April 2004 as the man interested used remote tactics on many levels including sexual intimacy and voice to skull initiation in remote communications.

It was not until the project became abusive did I report it accordingly. These men and their spouses are still at large in the music industry openly denying the event which transpired in many forms of abuse. The event was filed and documented in District Court witnessed by an ex NSA operative. Colorado areas were paid to overlook the event.

This band went so far as to incite their fans to commit a potential crime against me. Passing around a photo of me telling their audiences I am armed and dangerous and to report me to authorities or security if seen. This was deliberately done to put me in harms way. Why you may ask. Because the truth is a threat to these men and their illegal connections to mk abuse and signals related projects. After the event I did an interview and live testimony as a time capsule of truth to protect my civil and spiritual rights. This was done in case I was to disappear. A friend downloaded it onto the internet and was harassed by doing so. I believe it is still archived some where. I trust it was not hacked as the time display on the right is a way to identify the real time interview. I realize hackers these days can mess with this which is why I always suggest people use their intelligence.

Virtual space is a man made dimension using computer interphase which connects in from agent to target. Through these areas the bioelectric field which is silicon based is tagged and mapped. This data is later used to hurt or heal its subject depending on the agenda of the people involved.

The real to reel time is incorporated which communicates live intercommunications voice to skull and Memorex which can sometimes scramble signals and data. A virtual space in a man made timeless event. Remote viewing and visuals are created live and eventually mapped in computer interphase. Usually a target can be tagged via internet and later mapped and under illegal surveillance in their residence via satellite tactics.

Mind you I am about fighting the good fight. I believe in science beyond technology yet ascended technology and not the misuse or abuse of power which includes those in areas which are high profile.

I see this system or versions of being used as a frequency fence for behavior modification, prison or house arrest so to speak. Anyone the government red flags can be a target and eventually a victim of these assaults. One has to remember all those indoctrinated into media and governments including high level security or military are tagged in various ways. It is not what one does but how one does it. Once again the abuse factor which is a lot like THX 1138 and blade runner.

One thing I remember clearly during the initial two way communication the agent on the other side of the black screen typed in very clearly data on the keyboard which was converted on to my electromagnetic field in my secondary circulatory system to a point I would mouth the words voice to skull. I was entranced and rewarded with sexual surges by the agent or handler which by the way was mutual and live.

Eventually my secondary circulatory system was digitized and mapped into a signals communication and radio wave beyond quantum and more than a spirit of the radio. I was then communicated live voice to skull and was isolated and harassed out of my residence 2004 which was the beginning of a very intense ride.

I know my Multidimensional gifts and channeling abilities which are more than sacred. I am amazed at the concept of those who abuse the honor to communicate in many forms including what I am able to do.

With the right beings involved perhaps the event would have been more aligned with Spirit. I did everything to keep the light and unconditional love running on my end yet the constant barrage and abuse by the handlers and programs became a bit too much and became obvious their intent was malicious and personal in a more than negative way.

Tagging systems in virtual space on electromagnetic fields. Fly by assaults

Tagging systems take on many forms and are used for various reasons. Electromagnetic field tagging systems are done from a remote distance or cloaked in a fly by. Hidden tracking systems are used while the target is evaluated from a far before the operators tag their subject. People become targets for many reasons. Sometimes there is a personal interest. Star seeds are an attraction especially if they have a special ability or gift.

Scientists contracted with government projects are tagged, observed and sometimes interfered with never to truly have their serene moments of brilliance as much of their discoveries are still clouded by an iron hand.

Many people can become targets for a hidden agenda such as Manchurian candidate or covert operations. John Lennon a perfect example of someone under the influence of an mk assault in hearing controlled and monitored by government, the affect a Manchurian opponent programmed by government to take him down.

When I was tagged in 2004 April I was interconnected in a virtual timeline or illusion of real time. My electromagnetic field was tagged and a virtual live feed and holograph via satellite drove my virtual suit. The event and mapping opened a two-way communications system and live feed between me and the handler. The experience beyond intimate and sexual which was obvious to me this man had a personal interest.

The virtual space usually monitored and mapped remote from a computer vitals included. I remember how easy it was to communicate at a remote distance. The distant healing work I had done in the past affective and powerful of which many clients would comment on in color and vision.

The event in April 2004 of which I was interconnected live in a session with what I will call the handler involved a man in a headset sitting on a chair in electric blue. The session contained me removing templates of which I extracted extremely fast in virtual space. I informed him these templates contained trauma of which he did not need to hold on to any longer.

I also removed his helmet in his etheric design and told him he no longer needed this with me. The experience started off like a distant healing session and became sensual, sexual and digitized. This was not the norm for me in a session as I never mixed intimacy with my clients. I remained lucid in the event. The next day I made a note of it in my journal and communicated it to a close spiritual sister of mine. I felt intuitively I helped this man and left it at that. Shortly after I was tagged via evening and became interconnected in the experience which altered my life.

Virtual space is indeed fast forward and high speed. When a natural telepath gets plugged into the machine and agent interphase everything moves quickly. Mappings are done voice to skull in wave modulation and affects are activated. I was aware of being plugged into something machine based in communication live to the agent. The experience was a virtual mapping, and beyond digital. Virtual dream pool collectives are created in such a way. The experience can create the illusion of immortality yet one must remember it is a machine based telepathy program and not ascended machine based technology. The experiences are simulations of false realities which can create warps and tears in the electromagnetic field.

Colorado and California are hot areas for virtual games and mapping via internet and machine interphase voice to skull. Most people are mapped while using their computers. Scanning and digitizing also transpires. As mentioned many people in the entertainment industry use these technologies for their personal recreation and intimacy.

Fly by taggings are done in a cloaked environment such as the simulation environments I was exposed to. Many black satellites are used to scan and measure light in the electromagnetic field. I remember clearly feeling pressure on my chest cavity as the initial tagging took place.

It felt like a remote laser attaching on to my secondary circulatory system or Merkaba. The Merkaba generated by light consciousness and ones spiritual lifestyle. The pressure in my chest cavity was obvious. I remember lying in my bedroom the whole time interrogated voice to skull in what felt like hate and static coming from an outside force.

My secondary circulatory system tagged onto their radio wave began dancing to music. In the beginning of the interphase I was moving my energy myself of which they became interested in. Especially when I meditated or unified my chakras. Their instruments could detect and measure my electrical circuitry and Merkaba in expansion of which I suspect they had a need to control with a more than selfish agenda.

The secondary circulatory system goes beyond bio electric into photon electric. In vision digitized visuals of black, white, red in movement with a live agent communicating with me.

The dream pool collectives are used in covert projects beyond area 51. Most people are mapped to some extent when they dream. From a distance the light is measured and the attraction from an entity will be apparent to those who have sensitivity or are magical practitioners in some way.

There have been times in the past when I have felt a remote scan prior to this event. It felt like a heat signature with a slight burn and quite brief. Other times I remember seeing parallel dimensions and bleed through with entities moving through hunting for a target. I would quickly get up and clear the area with sage and other esoteric techniques.

When people become tagged or pulled into these projects there is a satellite driven interphase and communication mapping ones brainwaves. The images can consist of many things in between the spaces such as cartoons, digitized people, handler and whatever else they decide to throw in along with the psyche of the target. For me I found it easy to move the pictures back and forth which I became quite good at it. The agent and I were in a fast forward communication as other handlers were interconnected

Most people I feel would not know what they were exposed to if they were tagged by such systems. Knowledge is power. I am sharing accurate data with you as it may perhaps give you clarity and protection in the future. In the past my visions were always lucid pure with 100% clarity.

With the machine interphase in communication I was well aware of the agenda in conversation. The mapping on my fields and brainwaves were obvious. Later these mappings and tactics would be used in attempt to add, delete or modify the conversation and interrupt my meditations deliberate.

As in 2004 the program kept me in a space of trauma. I remained awake with no sleep hearing in communication the constant verbiage of interrogation. I was interconnected and would take a journey around the world in a cloaked communications system in hearing with live agents. I stayed more than positive and love based during this experience as best I could. The frequency fence so to speak was something of a personal prison created by these operators of which I did not belong nor was warranted in their actions. Yet was obvious to me how these projects were used in the past and the false now.

As mentioned I see the benefit and the curse of such technology. I saw the dark side of the operation in experience yet was well aware how this could change to a positive overnight. Tagging systems are used on military and high profile people without a doubt. The down side is the handler in communications and the agenda which can be a detriment. One is at the mercy of the virtual agent and lie as they will show and tell them what they want them to see and hear. This is a complete violation of Spirit.

Children can become victims of such programs and end up on more than milk cartons. Mk related programs can and do abduct children of which many people are oblivious to. With technology such as it is used today there is no reason why any crime can go away unsolved. I have experienced enough of the remote communications to know this technology and can tell you big brother sees it all.

Yet the bigger multiuniversal eye in the sky always overshadows crime in the underground and in the end the virtual lies which have no foundation dissolve along with the entities they create. We are interacting with mutiuniversal consciousness daily. With these projects man made interdimensional entities are created by virtual programs creating false dimensions which have no validity in any universe. These areas driven by a false ghost in the machine can affect and be a detriment to many unsuspecting unless one is educated or up to speed in science and mysticism. High tech wars are being used on the unsuspecting and have been used in government and military for a long time.

Symptoms, false diagnosis and brainwashing tactics, electronic dissolution of memory, implants and devices both seen and unseen. Silent detection.

9

Symptoms regarding a neural remote assault program can vary depending on the severity of the case and the psyche of the individual. Schizophrenia, bi polar diagnosis are an almost certain form of an mk assault broadcast or entity intrusion. Sometimes this can be an actual parallel bleed through from a legitimate past or future event which connects into ones soul extensions however in such cases soul descension/extensions do not operate that way. Soul descensions are fluid and high frequency in light language consciousness and part of ones Ascended Mastery.

Symptoms can be many: Ringing in ones ears, high pitch frequencies, sensing and feeling a presence, odd sleep patterns and hearing voices. For most mystics this is the norm in so far as we are used to navigating in many universes simultaneously however the man made influence of machine based intrusion and mk tactics are obvious and easy to detect for those of us well trained off world so to speak.

For the average bear they would not understand the dialogue or intent and would not know how to deal with it. The voice to skull in communication is done in a silent transmission of which only the target can hear in frequency.

70

Once the mapping and electromagnetic field tagging is done and interphased onto a satellite driven computer link the event can lead to remote assault tactical warfare which includes an almost animatronic movement in body and reflexes, mental conditioning and feedback programmed by the handler.

War criminal tactics are used if the target fights the assault as frequency fences are used to create a kind of contraction in the design or body something which feels like a g force.

This tactic was used in my case done by a group of men and their counterparts in California, Colorado and Canada 2004-2008 plus or minus. Still at large in war crime activity.

As mentioned all beings are psychic. The more advanced we become the more we attract opposing forces. It has been my experience the opposing forces are government oriented and in my case was a personal attack which was originally done on me using a machine based fly by tagging in live remote. The sexual intimacy initiated by a high profile male in entertainment.

Later on an added dialogue and interrogation voice to skull created by their reptile in consciousness wives who were their counterparts driving the crime.

It was very clear what was me and what was not. I used my Ascended Multidimensional Mastery in consciousness and Merkaba as a benchmark. My experience as a professional mystic and multidimensional channel also gave me clarity and protection in these areas.

There are many High Priestesses who channel or draw down which of course works in resonance with ones space suit in alignment with Spirit. Covert tactics attach a communications system on to the channel to open a medium in which they can communicate. This tactic takes advantage of the true telepath.

The voice or intruder can take the form of an agent wearing many masks from god to relative, demon or whatever it knows will provide a reaction or response. The brainwaves are mapped and a voice modulator is used to create anything from cartoon visuals to remote viewing and telepathy tactics. Forgive me if I repeat the same data throughout this book. I am my own editor for the most part and sometimes reflect in parallel the same event. Enough said.

Sometimes the visuals are sent from a computer interphase and other times a real person or live agent. This is done in transmission and receiving. Constant conscious remote communication is done non stop with a feedback mapped onto ones brainwaves and vitals.

My Merkaba secondary circulatory system mapped, tagged and assaulted creating a rhythm and light later to be mocked in the form of a book written by the handlers wife or in this case his partner in crime. I choose to reiterate this event as the people in association are guilty and held accountable for this act.

Many professions or so they are called in psychology have no concept of these projects. Those who do are driven by the all mighty dollar and would rather get paid entertaining the illusion at the cost of the target then resolving the affect created by such warfare. It is easier for them to medicate the situation as a quick fix then to heal the being in crisis.

For any cult to brainwash someone is to take them away from that which they love or are empowered by. Cults by the way take on the form of sick governments, religions and anyone who is obsessed with the illusion of power. Unfortunately Wiccan covens receive a bad reputation of which is not warranted. There is good and bad everywhere however my experience with covens and mysticism is harm none as we do not knock on doors to recruit or use mind control to influence another. Grid protection yes.

With a voice to skull assault program tactical warfare is a typical military interrogation intelligence spy technology. Isolate the target, tag and map brainwaves attached onto the hard drive of the operator and agent. Use psychological driving tactics from remote visuals to communications in negative concepts racial slang, hate driven remarks mapping rem and creating a voice to skull mapping of everything which is viewed through the eye of the remote.

Non stop negative chatter does not get positive results of which they know. The experience parallels many science fiction novels in so far as spiritual censorship and control programs go.

Sexual assaults are done by surging chakras mapped by the machine driven technology. Once again this is done by a live agent or handler. Machine based telepathy in conversation is later on used to continue the assault on the target by manipulation of the conversation. The outcome created by the sexual intrusion onto the target is an output of one desensitized in experience regarding sexuality and relationships.

An interrogation 24/7 is done using a false government NSA/FBI/CIA database manipulating the conversation from names to anyone or anything which once again can create a response. Anything viewed through the camera eye is mapped, narrated and catalogued behind a dark screen hidden in an underground of a wireless communications system.

Used for recruitment into anything from government agents to sex slaves both male and female which does not exclude children, Manchurian candidates to drug runners and of course terrorists. All done by yes our nice governments driven by their Satan which is indeed a false god equating to mans negative ego using machine as the driver.

Christians invented Satan fact 101. The only demon I have ever witnessed is that which man and the evil developed by his own mind and intent create. There is no entity in the name of Lucifer to blame on this one folks. The driver is indeed man and the misuse of technology in the form of a weapon.

The covert technology can play quite the sexual predator in the room of a little girl that does not know there is an uninvited guest or tea party taking place using mk related assault tactics in remote. The next thing she will be having lucid dreams and sex with a real man hidden behind a mask and a black screen and her parent will not have a clue.

Children on the internet today are tracked in silent communications, mapped and catalogued. Heaven forbid these men or women get a hold of one of them for a potential candidate for sex or their own personal entertainment. With an mk assault they become programmed into sexual slaves and are mapped to experience pleasure with their handlers. This is not love based by the way anything but. It is control based.

This is the ugly dark side of these projects. Entertainers in the music industry are more than corrupt and over indulging in this remote tactical assault program. They play the victim yet they are indeed the stalkers getting away with their crimes as they have dark government ties in the underground.

I personally do not recommend anyone having contact via internet with people in the entertainment industry. I have experienced first hand the sexual games and abuse in remote assault tactics used. I feel sorry for anyone contacting the people I had more than intimate communications and experience with. They are in reflection sexual predators and abusers which includes their wives and children.

These projects have cost people their lives and families. Many in the industry of music and entertainment are in denial regarding the murder of their own families using these mk related tactics. It is much easier to forget than except the truth.

Incest in the industry is obvious using remote assault tactics. Virtual machine based interphase in communications is created by sexual intimacy. Many men in the music industry use these tactics to tag potential girlfriends or whatever their needs are in the moment reflecting their internal sickness and more than a disease.

With electronic dissolution of memory, memories can be added or deleted using these same warfare tactics. Hence mapping of ones electromagnetic field which includes the aura can be used as a weapon as the tactical affect would be to use that being as a communications system running programs into the field of the target.

Many Manchurian candidates have no recall of what they do which is part of the convenient government way of cloaking their crimes hidden in the silent assassin. Memories in visual or conversation cannot and do not replace experience at the soul level in any form or universe.

There is no such thing as disease as all disease is frequency based. Alzheimer's is a perfect example of electronic dissolution of memory and the affects long term of abusive tactical warfare systems can create. We have technology when used in alignment with Spirit which can heal overnight and can transcend this blue world for the better.

This technology has been available for centuries and beyond the illusion of time. It is encoded in every cell and atom of our DNA and is true Ascension and frequency based. There are many who fear this transition into full light consciousness.

Merkaba or multidimensional mastery in consciousness ones Celestial and not human heritage breaks down the foundation of lies driven by the shadows of a false government and religion for centuries. Their solution to oppose this knowledge is mk assault tactical warfare.

Yet they are the first ones to covertly experiment with celestials and their abilities and map the unseen using stolen devices and technology based on a species not from Gaia.

Ascension is based on Celestial Heritage which erases the illusion of what people see and hear from day to day in all forms. Telepathy is for real and should not be disrespected in any form. The abuse of which I have witnessed in the attempt to torture a soul is inexcusable in all universes and the repercussions of those doing these crimes equates to no ascension to those doing the assault as they become slapped on the petre dish end of story.

I have had many discussions pertaining to my experience with Elders and Mystical clergy. As High Priestesses and Priests we agree there are many forms of intelligent energy which can create the appearance of many things.

I embrace all forms of energy in consciousness. All experience is sacred, not to be described or influenced by a remote handler in conversation used to control for their own personal entertainment. This includes the sexual power of the High Priestess.

The illusion in concept regarding division of ones hemispheres in the brain is just that as there is no separation or segmentation in any form. Ones hemispheres are balanced in a harmonic and can synchronize and merge into full light consciousness even through an event such as an mk related assault. The multidimensional channel is always running energy from multiuniverses. The body is holographic and multiuniversal and protected in form.

The concept of the High Priestess containing an alternate personality is not driven by an mk assault or tactical warfare. To those who map such beings are once again disrespecting the mystic, spirit in many forms and the channel.

The astral planes in dimensional form have transmuted and ascended through planetary ascension which includes interdimensional and interstellar space. The affect is multiuniversal consciousness or consciousness in motion.

Any so called astral debrea floating about in many circumstances is created by mk assault warfare and false dimensions, a parallel bleed through created by a man made rip in dimensions beyond space and the illusion of time forged by psychological warfare attacking the spirit or soul which is immortal.

Implants can take on many forms. With an mk assault type project they take on the form as words or suggestions repeated in disrespect in a silent hearing to the target. Their opposite of a prayer or mantra for example. They create a polarized opposite in negative of the target which has no connection to any dimension. This is by the way considered unethical and a form of silent torture.

These are dissolved by affirmations and light languages as well as frequency based harmonics using many forms of healing systems which include machine and hertz based frequency repair. Photon sound beams are used for cellular regeneration and can assist as a support as ones entire body and consciousness responds to light.

Raising ones vibratory rate and channeling the event in a positive direction, overriding and deleting programs using the Metatron wave is more than affective for transmuting.

Ceremonial healing and running of grids will assist in fortifying ones space. My Merkaba heals and regenerates on all levels. My abilities as a healer have always repaired a lot of potential damage done by many forms of intrusion either man made or otherwise.

Other implants can be created using a fly by tagging or magnetic induction which can create a remote controlled mechanized affect in the body of the target. This is done using technology at a remote distance usually initiated by a black satellite or cloaked craft.

From my personal experience the assault program went beyond a radio signal and electronic torture and was indeed beyond quantum. Nano technology can be used as a benefit to all beings when used correctly in so far as allowing ones spiritual consciousness to affect the healing and design.

Haarp projects can be used to affect and manipulate at remote distances yet usually these devices do not tag individual targets rather a collective in cities in synchronized feedback and mapping.

Most of this technology does not have power unless one allows it to. The tactical warfare which tagged me personally was indeed a different animal and invisible beast in government warfare. It is more than abusive and unfriendly.

My Merkaba or secondary circulatory system attracted a lot of attention by MIB types which became obvious as it is measurable in pulse and light harmonic. The tagging used which attached my field onto a propulsion and radio signal was done in disrespect to not only me yet Spirit in all its forms and designs.

My Merkaba was attached onto engines from motorcycles to musical instruments, radio signals false heartbeats and of course used so they could communicate via keyboard in programming courtesy of a man in California. At first as mentioned I was loving, accepting and open hearted to the positive experience of using such technology merged with my being for the higher good.

These entities called people are connected to dark operations which promise them immortality based on the illusion of machine driven technology and the misuse of. The men involved in my assault were clearly Nazi oriented following in Hitler's footsteps, goose-stepping all the way. They radiate nothing but hate in many forms which equates to fear and will stop at nothing to drive their agenda using people as human shields.

Of course people and the concept of human is just that as there truly is no such thing, We are spiritual/soul celestial beings encased in a matrix which through light body and DNA activation shifts into Merkaba and multiuniversal travel in consciousness This is why the mk assault tactics are more than offensive to Spirit.

One can say perhaps from their perspective they are trying to do something positive even if it appears evil. I can tell you this is not the case. These people are what I would call a low reptile decent with no heart chakra and no spiritual evolution. They attack or are attracted to those that are only to map the consciousness of the being in more of a psychological fashion null of spiritual insight.

They remind me very much of the war criminal scientists and torturers of WWII. The sad thing is it is clear to me they are not connected to full light consciousness for if they were they would not feel the need for such actions. True Ascended Celestial species do not feel a need to dominate the other as they are all connected in to the Multiuniverses of Ascension.

These people in their machine consciousness in entity form are empty and void of spirit. The people connected are a reflection of this hence their dark agenda will fail. Brilliant minds of the past that have departed this world and perhaps were something of a negative in their perceptions of others understand their experience after they leave the planet; they realize the negative ego and evolve. It is unfortunate these people have to die to get it. With the agenda in technology their machine promises immortality in the name of the beast which is man in machine. They are being lied to however and will become trapped as a false collective. This goes for the entire new world agenda.

Those with true ascension coordinates will be phase shifted and bi located. For more information regarding Ascension read my book Transmutation through Ascension soul of the son. I am amazed at the negative control mechanisms intruding in ones fields with these tactics. It is from my experience they are terrified of one shifting into that which we are meant to be in light body form which is more than electrical and photon electric and advanced machine technology...

High tech security projects and covert programs targeting civilians

10

In these times it is more than clear the exaggeration of security measurements to promote fear in the masses. It becomes more than a circus and sometimes a joke with the way propaganda works. Television and media of course show no integrity and appear non valid. Everyone knows they are censored in every form whether people realize it or not.

Surveillance cameras are everywhere. From black balls reflecting the spying eye to photo radar. Blue tooths are used to map brainwaves. The masses are now conditioned to be programmed by machine based intrusions and for many it will be more than subtle and influential to a point they will not realize it right away. They in refection are fear based and suspicious of anyone in their neighborhoods who does not have an American flag hanging in their front yard.

The entity or agenda in form is simulating a mock revelations hiding behind the mask of Christianity and even demon worship to create the affect. These organizations reflect a hate for anything spiritual in any form. Yet the monster created was by this very organization.

Psychotronic warfare and aerial tactical assault mappings go on every day. Most people are oblivious unless one becomes a target or gets caught in the crossfire. Beings such as myself have a natural antenna which pick up on these black satellites and the transmissions.

With 911 big brother now has an excuse to go door to door sniffing around. In my experience the mk assault including black ops programs archived my experiences as well as mapped my fields on all levels. The project itself is used for a recruitment of some kind. This includes machine based telepathy which encompasses remote viewing and wireless communications and training etc.

The program shape shifted into many forms. Many times sexually intimate which is how they controlled me at first. Later on it became more obvious and hate oriented especially when I protested the fact the verbiage in hearing was not appropriate in so far as the way I was being manipulated and abused in remote.

It is obvious to me the agenda started in full affect after 911 as that was a trigger for this order to make its move, in 2004 I was tagged and intruded upon after I sent my book to a high profile musician in California which of course one can see my interview about. This man and his brothers so to speak are tied into this regime. They have enough government underground contacts to get away with what they are doing which has been going on with them for at least thirty plus years. Most people are aware of the dark side pertaining to the misuse of technology. The affects lingered after WWII and of course centuries prior.

The technology stolen by the Nazis extracted from many brilliant souls tortured and experimented on. As well as the fragmentation of a lower ET technology which is what Hitler wound up with to sway the masses. Hitler of course a programmed entity which was clearly reflected in his eyes and mannerisms.

There are many archives surrounding this planet which reflect the true history of Gaia. Not man's version or an mk ultra program yet true Celestial species which seeded this planet.

The future in parallel of the Nazi regime never vanished. There was always an afterimage and the misuse of technology not to mention the war criminal torturers who managed to find sanctuary in these areas and not by coincidence. The so called elites cloaked in many guises waiting to launch an attack in the name of their leader.

A simulated Atlantis to some extent as the misuse of power and technology was clear. A pattern paralleled.

Opposing species not advanced in technological areas started a war with the Celestials which were archives for advanced machine technology and the DNA template of true Atlanteans and multiple species.

Atlantis I might add had many ports or multidimensional gateways of which were interdimensional and multiuniversal. Advanced species connected in unison.

Later to be phase shifted and bi located. The power on Atlantis was a specific race of beings of which I am pleased to say are not Aryan decent. Hence the parallel flip flop.

I went through a rather intense experience pertaining to Atlantis which I will not cover in this book. The event was years prior to the assault in 2004 which I keep separate.

Yet to give one the idea power struggles have been the basis for most wars. Religion is just a mirror. The energy in consciousness represented or harnessed in magic is real. Faith and knowing, knowing and experience. Experience into doing. Energy in motion.

Magic and vision seen through the eyes of a true mystic, scholars and scientists are always of infinite value and of course a threat at the same time. Since the beginning consciousness and soul/spirit is what drives the vehicle. With true ascension the Golden Path becomes real.

Governments lurking in its shadows are the first to deny Spirit and ones connection to celestial heritage yet they are the first to show up with their stealth technology to tag and cloak the target when it becomes a truth and the light measurement and abilities become obvious. Such as what transpired with me.

The Shadow Government boys club of course are the record keepers for the history of man and his version of. Plus or minus the murders, tortures etc. they did to acquire their data.

In these times which will be challenging I would say stay spiritual and fear nothing. Do not believe what they tell you for it will be a lie. Trust Spirit and your intuition. In these times we shall see many swept away.

My sense in knowing is they are frightened for the future of which they cannot change. I for one am not. I do know any simulation of a race in projection will be a shadow government program.

I do know true Celestials are real and are part of ones souls' essence of origin which is a spiritual birthright no one thing or man, machine can take away ever. This planet is protected by a force unseen by any shadow government or god. This force can alter the course of man in a micro second.

Through projects such as these I remained in Spiritual tact and remained dedicated to my benchmark formed by my Merkaba.

All beings respond as a particle chamber and conduit for energy no matter what form. This is a universal given and a blessing. With True Ascension light body becomes Merkaba and is capable of Multidimensional travel through multiuniversal consciousness.

The programs such as connected to red helmet or mk ultra in many cases use radio hypnotic intercerebral control and a form of electronic dissolution of memory especially in cases where there is a strong need to control their targets.

I am blessed to have been in an ascended space in consciousness. This allowed me to decipher the psychological drivers and tactical warfare accordingly. I can imagine some people would not have been so lucky.

I remained in a space of unconditional love which was a protective shield to me in many ways. My background extensive in science and mysticism becomes a challenge to those on this planet who go by a certificate of false doctrine rather than believing and experiencing beyond faith.

Beings such as myself are targets for a reason. What we are psychically capable of is real and becomes an attraction and sometimes a threat exposing the truth in unseen languages. I believe the masses are ready for this truth. I believe the masses should see the horror of how these programs are misused and how tactical assault programs rape the spiritual design mapping the Merkaba or vehicle of light in disrespect.

If the agencies who tagged me in 2004 presented the real data uncensored the game would be over bottom line. They would be out of office and tried as war criminals. I wish to reiterate no one believes in the fusion of spirit and technology more than myself however this type of tactical assault is far too intrusive to ones unique Spiritual design. From my experience these people simply do not care if the soul/spirit suffers in the process.

911 emergency security systems
silent radar, covert intelligence

11

As mentioned earlier 911 was used as an excuse to misuse tactical warfare on innocent civilians without any just cause. When I was first intruded upon in April 2004, 911 was the man made live feed. The handler agent always referencing 911 with me. Numbers were communicated in code format and what reminded me of prisoner identification numbers or some form of serial numbers.

Colors were also prominent in remote as well as words and keywords, areas and locations.

I was interrogated about what I knew which was odd to me in silent communications yet it was my sense me being a true telepath and multidimensional channel in machine interphase they were more than curious.

It is obvious to everyone on the planet these days 911 was an inside job. I see the agenda of this order. I am clear on how they plan to pull it off. It will be using similar technology of which I was exposed to.

I was stalked out of my residence in trauma by these remote tactics. The Whitehouse plain and simple did not care.

An American civilian gets intruded upon and mapped in her own residence with high tech assault weapons in remote and no one does anything. A 911 event was what happened to me in Colorado in 2004. I am sure others will follow.

It is clear to me the masses are at risk and in harms way from an inside beast. Chemtrails and contrails mask the skies. The American people know somewhere deep in their hearts and ominous presence hovers above unseen yet felt and sometimes heard.

I believe all change is good yet at the risk of a blood bath I think not. Spiritual Liberty and Freedom and our rights are at risk without a doubt. I have to trust not only Spirit yet the good of all beings that regardless of the shadow there is the light which dispels it forever.

For the people on this beautiful blue planet I write a monthly newsletter pertaining to Ascension, planetary shifts and changes and this is a big one. It will present itself in a form of which the masses will not expect and change the collective overnight.

I would advise anyone to stay close to those you love in these times as one never knows when they will be taken away.

When the emergency response system 911 is dialed in crisis one expects to have access to an emergency contact which will assist them at lightning speed. 911 is of course an abused term. In numerology 911=11/2 is an esoteric Master number which deals with power in presentation and form. There is no coincidence these master numbers and dates are chosen in strategic political and military events.

The 911 terrorist Twin Towers episode in New York Cities attack was a statement of psi war in disguise. The advanced technologies masked in an mk ultra Manchurian candidate programmed by those hidden behind the scenes. The beast takes on the form and is used in a covert attack.

The silent communications system used by covert intelligence areas is and has been used in these attacks disguised in the yolk of a foreign intelligence. Deals made, a secret hand shake under the table.

I have always believed in the Law of Grace and Lady Liberty so to speak the true Spirit of America. With 911 an abuse of power was forged. Cause and affect rippling a vortex creating an excuse to clamp down on ones spiritual and civil rights amongst other things.

Americans are lulled and medicated by anything and everything from media to foods in which they ingest all part of the matrix in illusion. The true form in consciousness is advanced and beyond this illusion.

With 911 the media appeared out of line in disrespect to those who lost their lives as the event and images captured in reel recaps were more than extreme and in poor taste. Commentators feeding in excitement of lives lost.

I remember the silence of no activity as the world seemed to stop for a brief moment. There was an uneasy peace in the streets and an unusual lull.

I remember the flight path over my residence in Superior Colorado. Military jets were flying over the house. At that time it was a nice feeling to know I was protected as I sleep by the fighter pilot overhead. Never did I imagine I would be tagged and assaulted by an intruder using tactical warfare inside my residence 2004. I do have a strong sense my fields were being monitored and mapped at that time prior to 2004.

I do not blame these beings as there has always been a special place in my heart for those in military combat in protection of this beautiful land and planet. America was the spiritual pioneer breaking through the illusions to create the dream beyond it all.

The superpower and the true Ivory Dragon reflecting mysticism and science. Protected by wings of Grace in flight and a role model for other countries. I am not one who becomes involved in politics and religion yet it seems through my experience these two barriers collided of which I am compelled to address in universal truth.

I have always been flying under the radar so to speak. Doing my thing and minding my business teaching the language of light in many forms. The event for me was more than an unusual experience.

Surveillance and military sweeps engaged overhead using remote tactics including hearing and listening. This is nothing unusual yet after 911 there seemed to have been a false paranoia sweeping the planet in silent transmission. The masses frightened and vulnerable as sheep. The illusion and agenda of deception set in motion. For me as a Martial Arts instructor I believe in empowering the masses and making them as strong as possible including spiritually sound which takes on many forms.

The silent beast and stalker from my experience 2004 was the misuse of an mk related tactical assault and tagging computer interphase and system which appears non lethal yet in truth a lethal weapon in the wrong hands.

I believe there are covert areas recruiting beings such as myself for a psi war agenda which is to transpire in the near future. I clearly remember television media communicating clues of possible terrorists in ones neighborhoods which included white vans in the neighborhoods.

When interconnected live feed 2004 white trailers and satellite dishes were always pointed out to me. This included anything electrical, light poles etc.

Potential candidates would be trained in all areas in communications outside regular school rooms. Women were always of interest. The first thing I did when hit with this project was to contact the bad guys in government and say this is my name and social security number.

I am an American civilian who has been attacked inside my residence 2004. 911. I presented the names of people involved in hearing live feed and explained my Merkaba tagging. I do not believe in childish games and virtual lies. It is serious business tampering with ones powerful psychic mind.

I wanted to make these people aware of this as my mind powerful and sacred was not to be used as a toy to abuse. Nor my body which is my sacred temple. Yes I believe I can do things beyond miracles to benefit many on this planet yet not in the hands of those who show no respect for my abilities and contain an ill agenda. The NSA signals intelligence agencies have always been involved in wireless communications systems. Those of us who can make the technology work are beings such as myself.

I believe in remote piloting and if it meant to save or assist a soldier in combat I would be the first one to go for a true ride. I can be a remote spybird without a doubt. I realize there were too many agents involved in attacking me on many levels. I would not break or bend in consciousness as they would have liked.

I am more than a visionary when seeing our planetary future. One must spiritually ascend with machine technology in consciousness. I feel for what it is worth this civilization can obtain this.

I am optimistic pertaining to the future of man/woman so to speak which encompasses ones celestial heritage. Star Nations in celestial form must be anchored. All beings are telepathic and wired for this type of communications system due to our celestial heritage. The key is not to become a slave to mans illusion and the false machine.

Energy in consciousness can be mapped onto covert communications systems using satellite driven computer tagging systems. The technology replayed in feedback to an individual or the masses. Such as with haarp and other communications systems representing false messengers. These mock signals satellite driven will fail.

The true signatures are high frequency in light harmonic and take form in multiuniversal consciousness. Photon electric.

One thing I would like to mention. I am well aware there were good guys in these areas watching over me during this event. I wish to make this clear and apologize for those rotten apples who made their areas look bad.

Secondary Circulatory systems elf fields and light measurements, Merkaba 12

Merkaba esoterically speaking is a vehicle of light. Wheels within wheels in multiuniversal consciousness formed from geometric light languages. The body in form is carbon to silicon. Silicon into light body. Light body into Merkaba..

When the Merkaba is fully developed phenomenal power both internal and external is developed and generated. A true propulsion system activates, all chakras on a multiuniversal level are unified. Multidimensional gateways and doorways are opened.

Ones avatar abilities are heightened as the true telepath comes forth. This type of transmission in light frequency attracts Men in Black types or old Montauk boys so to speak.

Through my experience I did not feel a necessary negative from these entities more from those opposing my interdimensional communications with these beings who in representation appear as a form of extra terrestrials as they work in the shadows manipulating light waves and sometimes people for experimentation.

Not all negative I may add as they have access to technology which can heal by thought alone in pure consciousness.

On many levels I am able to be a multiuniversal translator for them which I sensed they were aware.

I have no fear of these beings as my Celestial heritage on many levels founded their technology and much of the knowledge they contain thus far. I know these beings well in interdimensional space as they are beyond the control of government or any known agency in or on this planet.

Shadow government intercepts and tags beings such as myself which can demonstrate a spiritual or special gift of some kind. The internal external war takes place. Most beings I have done counseling for who have been assaulted by a form of an mk ultra usually have special abilities which are obvious. They are extremely intelligent in some way and in most cases advanced spiritually.

An advanced form of spectral analysis transpires. Beings are digitized and archived. I do not find this a bad thing unless psychological warfare tactics are used. With a true first contact Celestials do not psychologically drive or psychically intrude in a negative.

There is an ebb and flow in communication. A true telepathy and an understanding beyond words felt unseen and easily measured in light. Multidimensional sight in visuals are clear and beyond machine based driven, manipulated or controlled.

They are pure light in consciousness and have no need to dominate or control in such a way. They represent a universal protocol in respect to all life forms which reflects in their communication through energy and transformation of. The Merkaba or vehicle of light acts as a circulatory system to the cardio pulmonary and respiratory system, a backup generator. Through Merkaba breathing or sacred breath one can create a primer to light body which regenerates the system and allows ones vehicle of light to expand.

As with the tagging my fields began bouncing all sorts of garbage on the radio as well as drum solos, guitar solos and anything else including voice to radio wave communications internal. If this is not disrespect to ones celestial being and design what is.

The original fly by night intrusion was clear and reflected an intimate mapping yet did not show its true form in harassment until later.

To me and anyone spiritual this is more than a universal no no even to the Men in Black beings off world. The miracle with Merkaba is onto itself . A vehicle capable of consciousness in motion and multiuniversal travel which is what one is designed to be. This of course becomes a threat to many cloaked in the madness of old world religions, government or anyone who is opposed to the truth in light form which is clearly measurable and provable.

There is no monopoly in the universe regarding universal consciousness and there never will be. It is in the best interest of these people and organizations to respect that which does not belong to them and honor the light and wisdom each being radiates.

I do wish to stress the sacredness of the Merkaba. It is a blessing to generate this propulsion in form and to those who attack or rape it with ill intent. I simply show no compassion. In kundalini the Merkaba is connected in yet not in full form.

In sexual intimacy a sacred union is formed by such a mystical force and intimate connection and not to be taken lightly.

True Telepathy and Mk related machine based intrusions 13

I have always been a true gifted psychic. In my earlier years I chose not to use the word psychic as in terminology the concept in its own has been misrepresented by many charlatans snake oil in hand.

Throughout my entire life and not only this one I have been blessed with an ability to spiritually heal, see with multidimensional sight and clarity and be able to activate DNA into light harmonic.

I never took this ability lightly as a matter of fact I respected my gifts, believed in myself and spiritually evolved and ascended into my divinity. I then encouraged others to do the same through my various eclectic teachings.

I have logged and confirmed more visions and prophecies than I can count. I have had more validations from clients I have done readings and healing work on as well as initiations I have done on my students.

When one has experience in these areas the mystical universe becomes the norm as well as natural telepathy and multidimensional sight or astral vision as some may call it which is indeed the process of being a clairvoyant, clairaudient and clairsentient being into full light consciousness.

When I was intruded upon in 2004 the technology was clearly computer interphase driven using my celestial superconscious mind as the telepathic driver. I do believe I can work miracles with this interphase yet at the hands of the beings involved it became more of a circus and a lab rat experiment in disrespect to my gifts and abilities.

Machine based or simulated telepathy is more than digital and is indeed a high speed super drive interconnected in ones psyche. I knew when first plugged in for myself in consciousness it was too easy in so far as they way things moved. At first I felt it was a new avatar ability, In a sense I suspect it is.

Simulated telepathy is real in a sense the true telepaths communications are mapped and interphased through a machine and another agent who can act as a witness, observer and record keeper.. Anyone interconnected into the transmission and frequency can connect in which transpired with me 2004.

At first I was excited and blessed to be in this space of communication holding no fear only love and trust for those I was in communications with. I was completely entranced in the machine based telepathy which was internal in a sense. I removed myself from most external conversation.

I believe this form of communication is the future unseen to those of us who can communicate on a higher level of ones divinity. I do not believe the communications system should be used as a toy for abuse yet it is my sense this is the wave of the future which of course the masses are conditioned for. Technology should not be used as a weapon bottom line. I was surprised to see the man involved in the intrusion done on me openly deny the truth. A disrespect to that which is sacred in spirit and proof they were abusing the right and privilege to obtain access to such technology.

The joke of it being it is my supercomputer mind and gifts that made it work in the first place which I am certain they were aware. To most people who become interconnected in these projects my advice is to document the visuals, communications and log them accordingly

Allow the conversation and moving pictures to transmute in light by the law of Grace. Most of the time remote photographs are used as psychological driving mechanisms.

Labels used verbally in hearing are created to distract the flow of consciousness and map the chaos so to speak. Feedbacks are played and a repeat program runs in a loop. The difference in remote visuals vs machine driven are many.

I have seen pictures as like a photo in remote and other times in driving a machine based miniature world. I became somewhat fond of this experience.

This reflects a military program in form. This program in similarity I remembered in my earlier years yet this time is was more enhanced in visuals and more controllable. It reminded me of what Nasa would use for their remote control robotic designs.

This is why I am convinced I can make this technology work the right way. I consider myself Ascended machine technology on many levels for various reasons and much due to my experience in the Celestial worlds of mysticism..

What I have noticed with some of the mk ultra assault projects is that the verbiage is abusive and visuals are not appropriate nor are they created by the telepath. The tactical warfare can be very harsh to ones spirit and soul which I deeply oppose. I am more than aware animals in many forms have been abused by such projects. Their light based minds assaulted which makes me quite sad especially when it comes to primates.

I would like to make clear we as a species are designed to ascend in consciousness which includes abilities beyond the veil of limited perception. When these abilities develop they are to be fine tuned and honored. Too many great minds have been intruded upon with no respect to the being residing in the form.

Many people who hear a voice in their head should think twice about the source of communication as some transmissions would be a normal clairvoyant experience and other times a remote controlled satellite tagging in communications using mechanisms and devices attached onto ones electromagnetic field which can map vitals and attack the physical design.

Tactics and programs using sound and remote pictures, psychological warfare and driving tactics. Remote Piloting

14

Much of the tactical warfare displayed and accessible in covert ops is a form of psi war and psychotronic programming. Once a subject becomes plugged in the technology is unlimited in so far as what can be tried on the target.

This includes all sorts of man made anomalies. The body becomes mapped, digitized and insulated becoming something of a spacesuit in a foreign land. Virtual machine eyes are mapped, connected and interconnected onto ones design. Transceivers and tracking systems are set through the elf field. A true AI warrior is created.

Specific colors and codes are used and at times associated with a program of some kind in subliminal feed. Other times the verbiage is communicated via live agent including specific information in code and visuals.

At a remote distance this can come in handy. The electromagnetic fields are mapped along with the psychic centers. Verbiage is used voice to skull in remote which replaces the psychic sensors as the target is queued to where he is on the map so to speak. Targets in remote are pointed out air and land.

When ones virtual eyes are plugged in remote telepathy is enhanced and a fighter pilot tactical warfare night vision beyond becomes easily available. One interphases in a space of virtual programs to some extent. The mind stays in an altered form of consciousness twenty four seven. In between the spaces of ones quiet mind is a program running.

A certain amount of conditioning transpires in military mode. The tactical assault programs in psychological warfare attempt to break ones confidence on many levels in order to isolate the target from spiritual support which can include family, spouse or loved one.

The target is removed from anything which can confirm their abilities and confidence. They are placed in live voice to skull feed assaulted and attacked in various ways. This is the dark side of these projects. If one fights the programs one is attacked in more of a covert form and the agents make an attempt to discredit what they consider a threat to their methods of abuse.

People or plants usually appear in odd circumstances to confirm what one is hearing or listening to and are usually part of the covert set up for those being targeted or recruited by the programs.

Much of this reminds me of A Beautiful Mind the story of John Nash which of course fits the mk assault profile right down to his diagnosis of being a schizophrenic. Many people are oblivious to the transmissions running rampant across the globe. Sensitives who are not developed will run to their doctor for drugs to mask symptoms of an unseen atmosphere. It is always best to be educated regarding oneself on all levels to decipher such technology accordingly. Many times chemtrails or an X marks the spot will be seen clearly above ones residence. As transpired with me 2004 and not just once.

These fly boys made it obvious regarding their intent to get my attention. In Colorado one can not help but notice the military exercises going on. The vapor trails and con trails in the atmosphere. Their jets navigating the skies blocking enemy satellite signatures using a specific grid running formation at times. Other times cloaking an alternative psi war program in experimentation on the populous.

Sensor round can become extreme when plugged into some of these projects. What I noticed for myself was a definite need for the agent to maintain control and use unethical methods to do so. My emotional response at times became desensitized as I was in a removed space of communication. Though I would appear in public chatty and friendly in conversation I was always being intercommunicated with and intruded upon in a parallel mode.

These projects are clearly designed and used for high tech secret service security yet it is my sense not many of their agents are any good at these programs. Which in my opinion they were somewhat threatened by as my knowledge and ability to run with these programs was obvious and a success.

Much of the time was used in a negative space by these agencies as the programs could have taken a different course and more in alignment with a more ascended form of technology and science. I figured after four years of the abuse they would have sucked it up and honored my abilities and instead several tried to discredit the truth tongue in cheek even when they knew I have been correct about everything from the beginning.

It is my sense it went south because I was not willing to tolerate the negative abuse from these folks and decided to turn them in instead. I believe this is the ethical thing to do regardless of their status in the entertainment, government or military bottom line. Integrity goes a long way.

At one point I was informed by the handler agent via phone call on Maui and I quote 'if someone is hurting you in some way go to a sergeant or above and tell him what you are telling me.' I knew as well as he that was not going to fly as these agencies were all in on it so to speak and they would discredit me as fast as I came in to inform them. There were too many games being played and my life the cost. The local cop down the road would not bother to write a report and would instead make a mockery pertaining to any voice to skull in hearing. Yet the whole time they have access to these remote devices.

The question is how far is too far and how close is too close. Martial arts 101. Much of the entertainment industry uses virtual somewhat covert intelligence interconnected on the big screens and with those in entertainment. The sad thing is they are using these programs to commit crimes against the masses or anyone who they can entertain themselves off of. The media and entertainment just another poison arrow connected to forced religions and government.

There are many organizations which give true mysticism a bad name with their version of a false god. No true Cosmic Celestial supports their actions which are entity controlled and compiled from virtual lies. Blood money used to fund their dark operations which encompass low forms of behavior such as child pornography, group sex in the name of their gurus and underground occult sects which have nothing to do with any Celestial in any form. Sons and daughters are indoctrinated using sexual mk assault tactics and are raped on many levels promoting an untimely death. Mysterious accidents usually covered up by organized crime and dirty law enforcement.

I appreciate good movies as anyone else yet after the birds eye view of the entertainment industry and their behavior I am more awakened to the fact these people are on a downward spiral to nowhere as an entity collective.

Magazines reflect the ugliness of the so called community of actors. People forced to view a magazine tabloid in the grocery store checkout stand feeding the propaganda of these reptiles in entertainment. The same old circus of actors and their 'issues' all interconnected in organized crime and not worth much when it comes to universal consciousness and Spirit.

These entities who think they have a free ride to the heavens when in fact they are a trapped collective due to their contracts with mans version of Satan the true dead satellite.

Many of these actors digitized into a false immortality flaunting the illusion in blood money and negative behavior. To each his own yet not at the expense of an innocent being used for their own personal entertainment.

Such as what transpired with me in 2004. I was assaulted for their entertainment by sick organizations of high profile entertainers and their scorned wives. Motives concealed by organized crime and shadow government contracts and once again dirty cops.

The credible data shoved under the carpet and the 'entertainers' and their counterparts wondering about still taking remote pictures and committing crimes.

Conscious Remotes and Rem influence, sleeper cells

15

Manchurian candidates are targets programmed by world government agencies to carry out the will of an agenda. As with anyone in a high position of power or influence over the masses there is always an opposing force. Yet most of the time this force in representation is not created by a god more by a hidden organization with a covert agenda.

The good truly do die or shall I say transfer out young. Assassins take on many forms and with mk assault tactical warfare this animal is alive and running with sharp teeth. One will not hear much pertaining to the programs running as the cover-ups are usually done at the risk of another. I am astonished how no media touches the subject which is considered taboo and something of a mark no one wants with shadow government.

Those who have lived on this planet radiating truth and an inner light of awakening usually met with an early death due to the threat they created by those who have an agenda beyond the norm of society. Great minds take on many forms and identities.

They in consciousness live on in multiuniverses and star systems without a doubt.

Most taggings interconnect in through the dreamtime or an altered state of consciousness deep meditation, pranic fire breath or Merkaba meditation as an example. In the old days government would use psychedelics to connect in regarding red helmet projects or mind control. Religions of the day are no better in reflection as the witch hunts have always been ongoing though cloaked in a more sophisticated guise.

Now with mysticism and many involved in yoga and practices which are spiritual in lifestyle it is much easier. Music unfortunately has been used to affect ones psyche using a form of an mk assault and radio signals tagging which is quite a shame as the programs themselves are not a compliment to spirit.

I love music and will always be a rock and roll baby so to speak yet I can tell you to use discernment with music and those in the industry.

Certain bands in entertainment will stop at nothing for their own personal entertainment and agenda which is not in the highest good for those who are spiritual in consciousness and star seeds. Unfortunately I found this out the hard way. The sad thing is my gifts which are quite powerful were attacked in such an abusive way in disrespect. To know the predators behind the mask responsible is more than unsettling.

I attended a Nepalese celebration with a Lama one year in Boulder 2006. The woman singing had a somewhat piercing tone in her voice. The Lama looked over at me and said 'this music is disturbing your Spirit'. I smiled and replied yes how did you know? At that time I was plugged into a lot of the interconnected feed.

In any event it made me realize how spiritually unsettling it is for the spirit/soul to be attacked by a man made radio signal used for government interrogation.

Another time I attended a lecture given by a Buddhist Monk who was discussing the movie the Matrix and how he applied it to Buddhist teachings 2007 in Boulder.

I began to discuss AI intelligence programs with him. His background prior was computer science and AI intelligence. He was astounded when I communicated the mk signals assault programs and was interested in hearing more about it.

He was quite defiant in stating 'they cannot do that yet with AI' in so far as machine based telepathy and interphase dubbing the collective of the psyche onto the communications systems.

I smiled at him and nodded yet in my quiet mind said yes they can. Most AI Robotic technology is based on how to mimic so called human behavior. Yet through technology in misuse one can influence the 'human' to behave in a semi remote altered state robotic through machine interphase. You may ask where the soul dwells during such a merge.

Depending on the severity of the assault the soul spirit will evacuate the mortal design. Other times it anchors in with soul extensions and maintains a pillar of light such as what transpired with me. One may hear the term walk ins as these entities usually have an interconnection to experiments within the realm of these hidden areas.

Many science fiction writers wrote about this future which is the now as the technology has always been available yet cloaked in the shadows of controlled experimentation. I respect these beings reflecting our planets future in true vision.

I realize through my spiritual evolution and the abilities of which I contain much of who and what I am was merged onto a communications and advanced computer system. I also realize we are the celestial star seeds we seek and the technology resides within every cell and atom thus thwarting ones spiritual evolution into ascended machine technology not used to control or manipulate yet reflect the celestials we are. In respect to all tribes and nations which is indeed true ascension.

As mentioned earlier sleeper cells are used as a stasis in so far as programming beings for whatever agenda needs to be carried out. You will see a lot of the so called terrorists indoctrinated by planetary government using tactical assault programs which influence tag, control and manipulate. Voice to skull guarantees them a journey to meet their false god. They will think and believe they are talking to god when in fact they are talking to a shadow agent behind a machine in programs. A dark area to say the least. This is the beast I came to meet in 2004 which of course reflects the false god of a man made agenda.

With the constant interruptions of an mk assault ones spirit becomes intruded upon. Alternate programs run in visuals and verbiage and much of the programs feed and drive off of the true telepathy of the individual.

It is mans way of trying to capture spirit in consciousness. Summoning the man made minion in reflection to do his will. This minion has no power yet the communications and tagging systems can wear beings down especially if they are unable to identify the source of what is attacking them. Transceivers and advanced signal broadcasting is hard to detect and most civilians would not be educated enough to figure out what it was they were hearing and listening to.

To many this invisible beast will reflect anything and everything. This is the affect they wish to create. I have had targets contact me in the past affected with a form of a signals assault program. Their eyes when tracking and object would move much like typewriters and trigger with certain key words used. They would be driven by 'the voices' telling them to do this or that and would follow and trust that communications system.

They would in turn wind up in trouble though innocent falling victim to the programs. I would council them not to listen and document what was being communicated. With my tagging it was different as the agents wanted me to know who they were and were somewhat arrogant about it. I was very much on to them and did not allow the illusion to go on for too long as soon as I realized the agents were stringing me along.

105

It was a sad event however as it cost me my marriage in the beginning due to the trauma and interconnectedness of it all which I was enveloped and controlled by in remote.

One thing I wish to mention we are working time out of mind beyond quantum physics. We are capable of manifesting our multiple realities by thought in light consciousness. With True Ascension comes unlimited freedom. This is not religious based. The energy in consciousness is why I was tagged and my mind in consciousness was used as a weapon vs their machine collective. Happy to say I believe I won that bout.

In some cases of psychological torture and driving using a covert silent communications the mind, right and left hemispheres are balanced and unified normally. The brainwave mappings in conscious attack and assault in remote conversation gets mapped and a recorded interphase and feedback 'answer already provided' gets replayed in a continuous feed. This includes an attempt to insert, add or edit ones thoughts picture and photos included. All psychology based.

For many people I suspect segmentation would take place in the psyche and alternate personalities would come forth to cope with the assault and trauma of the event.

For myself being a multidimensional channel and anal when it comes to being in control I refused to take a back seat to the agent or machine interphase. Especially when I realized it was assault and abuse driven and not spirit or love based.

I refused to be told who I was in its eyes and their version of and how or what 'it' thought of me nor did I believe in the voice modulations of my deceased mother talking to me which I clearly communicated to the agent in reflection of their disrespect to her design in consciousness, spirit and energy. They use any tactic they can think of which is indeed a model of yes the movie the 'Terminator' Mysticism became a weapon. Anything I did empowering was a noted threat by their intelligence agencies. A mockery was made in the name of any god in disrespect to me and my sacred temple body was communicated. Remote attacks were constant and done by tactical warfare operators in various areas. I can

106

compare it in some ways to electroshock therapy for example when one defies the communication there was a programmed feedback designed to interfere with ones brainwaves so to speak and a deliberate attempt to argue the correct statement which I would always communicate in thought back in full light consciousness which of course they argued even when they knew I was correct. My beautiful soul/spirit assaulted by these hate driven people.

These agencies and areas would gather intelligence data from various obituaries and people in conversation later to replay in a silent hearing. Racial comments were made and images of black men hanging from trees were visually communicated in remote in 2004. This is just an example.

This was done by a live agent mind you. Little girls and sexual innuendoes were also made and comments opposite of me in any universe and dimension were a constant. I would meditate and stay on my spiritual course and the more I would communicate affirmations the more they would interfere.

The agent from California at one point had the nerve to say 'the more you email the less we will listen' turning up the volume in remote abuse. Water boarding has nothing on these guys' folks. All done by remote, order less, tasteless and more than abusive and yes a war crime. This is the dark side of these people and their intelligence agencies which are not so intelligent by the way. In my circumstance the people involved were in the music industry and contained more than a history of remote attacks. I am well aware political parties and government agencies were all connected in to hitch a ride and take a turn abusing my celestial design.

California, Colorado and of course Washington at its worst. Not to mention Canada. Something perhaps the presidential candidates fail to communicate when they run for office in a convenient manner.

In the beginning I remained as love based as I could trusting in Spirit beyond faith which is what I believe I am more than protected by. No one ever wants to believe someone they respect at the soul level is beyond fallen and trapped in a false collective of evil, deceit and lies yet I was exposed to this very thing which left a bitter taste in my mouth by these men and their families. All this transpired simply because I sent a book on Spirit to one man.

My visions have always been pure and true. I have a reputable identity of which my entire life has been a reflection of. A spiritual benchmark of which they could not taint.

There are many areas in covert intelligence. My sense is I was intruded upon by several at once. I do intuitively connect in with the advanced species in forms beyond military black ops that are not the entity driven jerks as what attacked me from California.

I realize there is good and bad in very division yet it is up to those doing the good to take down these evil hate driven war criminals and the abuse they do onto ones spiritual design which is beyond unethical. As I mentioned the universe is composed of consciousness and intelligent energy which is more than spiritual regardless of ones belief in faith or nothing. The Soul in essence and form descends into the embodiment from the heavens themselves which are indeed beyond light years away and many universes and star systems. My celestial family and true heritage which no man or entity driven female can ever tear me away from. Throughout his story man/woman has hidden the truth of ones Celestial heritage which is not human.

He has stolen celestial artifacts sacred in energy and has deceived the masses in order to play the false god to control for his own agenda.

Power spots and grid lines in navigational interdimensional space are always captured or staked by military for control purposes. Anything which radiates a foreign or non human intelligence is of interest and of course torture goes along with this at times. The story of man is not so pretty when seen from the stars.

Through all these false realities created by these projects one thing is clear. Celestials have always ran and held the light on this planet. Those of us who generate light in powerful sacred ceremony, circles and gatherings to honor our unique design and celestial heritage why because it works that is why.

These programs and the men behind them are out of their league as the rest of the universes, planets and star systems are all merged into the true ascension wave with love, light, and transmutation of spirit leading the way.

The true Celestial watchers I represent in light and vision. I owe it to the beings of this blue world to communicate these programs as to not create fear yet to release that which has been trapped in ignorance and prepare the masses for any potential psi war which could transpire in disrespect to ones spiritual design and celestial heritage.

Consciousness in motion
true psychic kinetic activity

16

The stream of consciousness is a continuous flow of energy in motion. The force driving in a gentle flow is universal and fluid in resonance with celestial ebb and flow. Most Martial Artists can maintain this flow of universal chi or Ki which is an extension of ones aura and energy field. Ones mind is more than a powerful supercomputer in consciousness which extends into many universes and star systems simultaneously.

Kinetic energy is the body following this unique spiritual design. The confirmation from Spirit always defines the form. Those who violate this beautiful design appear fear based as the idea of an advanced Spiritual being seems to intimidate them on many levels.

I did the spiritual work ahead of time which I feel casts a reflection in so far as my determination of Spirit. I have been adamant about where I have been in consciousness on and off world which no machine or man can define in any lifetime.

Who I AM on this blue world in consciousness beyond form reflects how I communicate universal truth to all beings. My healing abilities as a Spiritual Teacher, High Priestess are more than powerful, and reveal a permanent imprint in multiuniversal realms, star systems and universes. This is knowing and experience accessing the multiuniversal computer in the full light universe. No ego involved.

My soul, over souls and many soul extensions in all universes weaved in the celestial fabric of Christ consciousness merged with Celestials. This universal knowledge cannot be raped or taken away nor can any intruder who demonstrates a witch hunt of ill intent against me borrow or steal that which I AM. Clearly stated. This goes for all life forms on this planet as all are interconnected in Spirit in a love based fashion.

The Blue Star Kachina is in representation Gaia or Earth Ascending into a star. This is not to be confused with the world government dead blue satellite archiving false data in collectives on the planet. Mans decoy to a false ascension. I do feel after my experience that yes change is necessary on a global scale as sometimes it takes devastation for people to awaken. The dark agenda of one world order however is incorrect as this will be taken down as it rises.

Gaia has archived this data back to Source in full light consciousness not man or woman. Those who surrender to a false signal will become more than trapped in the man made design. Man's machine with no voice, soul or spirit becomes a watered down version of Celestial technology.

True Ascended Machine technology is not connected to these agencies. The Celestial species is an advanced race in councils of light and does not support these tactics used by man on this planet. Those of us here on this timeline are Ambassadors of light and represent ascended machine technology which is why we are here now. The twelve cities rising from the oceans of universal consciousness in form is a silent communications system composed of multiuniversal translators with more than a first contact. For too long shadow government has played boogie man to the masses, creating false ghosts, voices and images. He will realize it is not wise to make a mockery of such things.

Energy in vibration and form can take on many overtones of Spirit. The entire universe is alive in consciousness as well as all living organisms in all universes and star systems. This energy like mentioned in my earlier chapters is intelligent and not harmful.

Since the beginning in the illusion of time man has attempted to write what he experiences observing this intelligent force. Interpreting ancient petroglyphs, sacred texts and of course old archives lost or stolen. Man rewrites his story as he desires or views it whether through divine eyes or a bent lens. What we are experiencing beyond description is no time in multiuniversal consciousness. We have always been able to navigate, bi locate and phase shift by consciousness and thought alone. This is ones true celestial heritage which what was taught by the Ancients.

Man has attempted to trap consciousness by creating time in illusion. Living by it he becomes a victim of his own design. He or she manifests cities by vision and imagination, cars planes, jets and other flying devices some by memories in higher consciousness.

Some believe when beings transfer or die so to speak they forget their lifetimes on Earth. It is my knowing this is not correct. All data and experiences are archived and merged into the full light universe for later access if one chooses. This goes for beings we love and knew as well as advanced technology. I truly believe love never dies as long as the heart remembers something of which my mother mentioned to me many times.

With True Ascension all data and multiuniversal knowledge is available each moment. Those of us who are conduits or Multdimensional channels access this data freely. It is used for education and of course navigation in consciousness, healing and multiuniversal translating.

There are hidden areas who seek beings such as myself for their own agenda and sometimes experimentation. They use man made transmissions to play a trickster to those who have a gift yet with true Mastery ones is able to see the trickster and know the technology which of course was my case.

I do believe the beings of which I was in contact with were psychic to some extent enhanced with machine based interphase and special affects which is another story. I am well aware there are many fanatic religions out there that have enough blood money to fund the abuse and misuse of technology in the name of their false god hence a not so holy war is launched.

I have communicated mk ultra to many types of beings and one thing stood out. The odd visuals reflecting a psi war tactic which became obvious the more I researched the event.

Many targets in California had images of negative pictures sometimes seeing themselves doing harmful acts to someone else. The being usually has no violent tendencies and is not connected to what some would call a demon in visual.

This is no demon, angel or minion. It is a tactical warfare program used on the masses and sometimes targeting an individual for experimentation. I knew a High Priestess who saw similar images and actually performed an exorcism against the entity in her residence in Boulder.

This entity I am more than certain wreaked of Colorado springs and military ops targeting mystics. There are many tactical warfare programs running rampant and of course depending on the agenda and the individual these people can be targeted keeping the church busy in the green performing that which is not a demon yet more an experiment and misuse of technology done on those who are powerful mystics.

They can in turn influence the masses by saying this is what happens when you work with the 'devil' which of course there is no such thing only man, mask and a misuse of technology.

Like I mentioned Lucifer consciousness has ascended. The whole agenda on planet Gaia has been about controlling information and power whether it is one person or an organized group of beings.

Witch hunts never faded away they merely changed form shape shifting disguised in the church or government seeking out potential threats to their illusion created which can debunk their agenda.

I am amazed to see so many people influenced by mainstream media which I must confess are my personal nemesis. I detest their illusions and the propaganda when we have the cure to all in the hands of this world. All illness and disease cured in the blink of an eye no war etc.

The planet such as I describe is here now yet no one ever looked with multidimensional eyes. Those who have seen it and know it such as myself become tagged.

Christ the Master was correct the Kingdom of Heaven is before us. It never left as magic is everywhere disguised and covered up by those defining power spots, sacred sites creating territories and covert military bases.

Any evidence of Celestials becomes cloaked as a Satan or god in some form. Later used and created as an object to fear in repent for acknowledging the species.

The keys lie in ones DNA through frequency and vibrational sounding. The Nazis of course were never a supreme race as they were a petre dish experiment of the Golden Giants, yet they in turn chose to target other beings such as the Jews and other races for mk ultra experimentation which took on many forms.

The Jews were not a chosen race. Perhaps they felt honored to be used in such a way as their DNA was experimented on. I can tell you it is not about a race or religion more a soul celestial heritage and telepathic spiritual gift and ability.

As a matter of fact Jesus was a celestial who taught DNA activation. He was not a Jew so to speak. Kabbalah is based on Celestial Angelic script which of course is not from here hence no one religion holds any claim on Spirit. Their Moses of course a prophet which comes in many forms yet as religions dictate they reflect mans version and personal will which is not based on True Ascension. My knowing is all religion and governments founded on false teachings truly need to fall and will.

Spirit in consciousness beyond science will ascend hence hold on for the ride everyone.

Man developed religion to control and manipulate bottom line. Religion has nothing to do with Spirit or true planetary ascension. As a matter of speaking religion is a barrier between worlds and dimensions which does not exist. All dimensions are merged into a higher universe in consciousness and light. Manifestation by thought is the key and pure intent which is truly all one needs to navigate in all universes.

The Annunaki a true celestial race are a species spiritually advanced and love based in light language communications. Anyone portraying these beings as the enemy needs to consciously connect into this species.

Man attempts to use celestials, extra terrestrials, demons, angels and gods to create an agenda representing their voice as his own. To some extent this can represent an aspect to oneself on a parallel dimension yet the true species has no connection.

A universal no no once again. The bigger eye in the sky is a force which will terrify the governments and any new world order on this planet. Not because they are bullies because they are real and represent truth with no fear.

We are extensions of these species containing a unique spiritual design and soul blueprint which of course is why there are those who oppose ascension. All will change overnight in full light consciousness.

I have been blessed to have felt the energy beyond the illusion of structure on this planet in frequencies beyond star systems, comets or meteor showers knowing the celestial energies and messages in all universes. A universal sounding and harmonic indefinable yet felt in unconditional love.

The mapping in 2004 desensitized me from that which I empathically felt in love on all levels. The experience felt more like a newly defined space suit such as an astronaut would wire himself to using my machines and theirs as the artificial life support and communications system.

The affect in driving an interconnected experience with visuals and a false knowledge at times.

Yet something was missing as with feeling and knowing at the soul level nothing can compete with experience to be replaced with a dialogue. A true merge with Spirit is feeling and experiencing love.

Masses have been taught from textbooks using incompetent lessons droned by a false knowledge for the most part. Society and their fears are a poor reflection in representation of their governments and religions. Thank goodness I was educated and trained off world so to speak. The poison of society today is the lack of dreams driven by pure thought or Spirit. The great minds of old guided by the stars is the truth of all things and a magic which will live in my heart eternal.

I have always been a magical being in more than one lifetime. Never had I anticipated such a harsh experience as was communicated to me. Through it all I remain steady in my pillar of light filled with Grace reflecting love within though shadowed by moments of defense and a bit lack of trust. I still believe and know what I teach by experience to be valid as all the practices of which I am dedicated to paid off.

Sometimes I truly feel as if I was merged off world and perhaps it would have been better for me to see this unfold from a parallax view in and beyond the heavens of that unborn world. To perhaps be seen in a future timeline. I said goodbye to many people I loved in 2004. Everything I held close to my heart was taken from me. Replaced by a dialogue interconnected.

Planetary shifts dream pool collectives and consciousness black ops mapping and cataloguing

17

As mentioned in my earlier chapters this planet in vibratory rate, speed and consciousness is ascending and becoming a star. As this transpires ones DNA activates and a higher level of consciousness and awakening transpires. Avatar abilities open up as one starts to mutate from carbon to silicon and from silicon to light body from light body into Merkaba.

This is a more than a powerful event and a once in a lifetime experience. It is a privilege to be alive on this planet during this transition. I do not feel it to be a coincidence for anyone on this planet to be here in the now as this event takes form.

Many covert areas including black ops map dream line activities and connect or shall I say interconnect into the mass populous.

I do not feel this is all a negative. I do feel there is a lot of cataloging going on. Light is being measured and cognitive brain wave functions are mapped to influence at night time or day.

From my experience I do not feel the Men in Black to be a negative more a protection yet that is just me. I do feel some dark areas in government who have no access to this area are attempting to interfere and create more conflict with that which does not need to be intruded upon.

It is one thing to have ones abilities mapped and measured and another to go through a traumatic mk ultra assault program for someone's entertainment or personal agenda.

I have always been connected into many species off world hence for me to be communicated to by MIB types was not an issue. It is more the imposters which give the credible species a bad name and rep so to speak.

Residing in Colorado a good portion of my life I was never intruded upon in a negative fashion by lower extra terrestrials so to speak or black operations. Give or take a few minor events here and there with visuals of ships in my bedroom before my eyes in a lucid vision at night yet vanished as quickly as they appeared. I would clear the place after the experience.

There were many times I would see parallel dimensions in my bedroom at night in visual at which point the room in definition would appear similar yet not the same. For example there would be a box or a lamp in the room and things would appear rearranged different.

Another time I experienced a type of entity black with tentacles enter my room at the bedroom door as if seeking something. I remember this event clearly as I was lucid looking up over it as the entity moved over my head and vanished into the wall behind my headboard. It glided as if it were on a plate of glass undetected. This same entity was seen by another woman of whom I have attended ceremony with in the past. I communicated this to one of my friends one night.

He proceeded to show me a picture of what he had drawn at her residence as my mentioning of the event appeared to trigger him in remembering the entity.

I could not have drawn the picture more accurate. The drawing and entity was just about identical to what I saw at my residence.

I do know the technology is out there. Interdimensional space and other dimensions are merging and those who are in tune with such areas see more than the average bear.

Entities and objects are brought in sometimes by ceremony and other times by covert projects running or traversing areas close in proximity. With Colorado Springs close by anything can happen. Yet with my experience it went way beyond that.

At times ones light from afar is enough to attract attention. As mentioned prior 2004 I remember clearly in definition what appeared to be a simulation room and a shiny black object which seemed to look like a prototype helicopter to use a better word and rather loud hum over my right shoulder. This all transpired as I lie in my bed at night. I was lucid and wide awake.

I was then interconnected into the machine interphase and remember the visuals black, white and red in a micro remote visual. Communications kicked in and all was in motion.

I simply contained no fear as to me experience in forms such as these is what I am here for so to speak. When in deep water become a diver so I believe. I had enough trust in technology to allow myself to experience the projects and beings of which are willing to connect with me.

Much of the mapping was intimate beyond sexual which later on was used as a control mechanism in verbal feedback responses by certain parties.

In the initial experience I felt protected and fortified. I had no reason not to trust the beings involved at that time. I realized later on when the communication was set in motion how things were to become negative and more a reflection of an mk ultra and less of the introduction to covert black ops communication which was more my natural wiring.

As mentioned this form of machine based telepathy can be used for anything. I am a natural telepath and multidimensional channel to begin with which made their programs easily definable through my spiritual eyes and knowledge.

I do not believe this event would have transpired to the level it has had I been anything less. I know how my Merkaba was amped prior and how they tagged my fields to their radio satellite signal.

This was abusive to say the least. At that time I was in an interconnected space of more than hypnosis and shock driven by mk ultra yet remained unconditionally love based and positive throughout the experience. I was completely engaged in the machine based telepathy in hearing and listening verbally mimicking my communicator.

Merkabas are sacred and not easily harnessed. They were aware of this I am certain and had an interest in mapping this force as well as measuring my light and abilities which were clearly in visual and obvious by their devices. Once again later on used as a feedback in my own fields.

My circuitry and spiritual wiring alone displayed to these people the way I used my Merkaba in healing and meditation which was interfered with on many levels and in disrespect to me and my practices.

As mentioned a drum solo live and guitar solo amongst other things were performed through my fields as well as the radio signal and attachment to anything on the regular radio stations. Music by a particular band and a few hypnotic songs were interconnected in to my fields.

The whole time an interconnected verbal narration of the event. Keywords were used live feed and later on reflected in print in their personal web sites, their biography books as well as their personal albums of the parties involved.

Heart beats were also overlaid onto my fields. This was abuse oriented and done in my sense out of maliciousness and not out of love. The experience I went through was a mix of many worlds in entertainment and military covert ops. From my experience the California group was more than abusive. Not to mention the illegal activity done in the privacy of my own residence at that time.

The misuse of technology is clear in my circumstance and the intent of the parties involved. Knowing the people behind the mask is more disturbing than the incident itself on some levels as the parties involved received no repercussions for their illegal acts.

I am convinced in knowing universal law takes care of the acts of those who appear to escape hate crimes such as was demonstrated later on by these parties. This is where I Grace and move on. Easily enough done unless the communications system is attached to ones fields and relays a constant negative feedback which was done on me as their way of harassment without a trace of their crime unless one is involved in these covert programs.

Your average Joe would not comprehend how ones brainwaves can become mapped to a point where the machine based interphase in communications can create a dialogue not based on the person being tagged or his /her own thoughts but by the agent.

This is an example of how they create an alternate conversation which reveals and demonstrates how people can become mis-diagnosed with a pseudo schizophrenic disorder or bi polar etc. to name a few. This in reflection is a nice government cover-up.   I always like to take an experience from its lowest to its highest. I am more than aware miracles can be performed by the correct use of advanced technology. I do feel in these times people are being mapped, tagged and catalogued for various reasons and not all positive.

Knowing the bigger picture of all things minus universal studios or a government agenda one can come to realize everything transpires for a reason. Even if the situation appears grim it becomes a catalyst for greater change within ones self at the soul level or on a higher level of ones divinity including planetary awakening and consciousness.

Not all of these programs are negative. There are many covert projects which are fighting the good fight so to speak. I believe with my experience there were many looking out for me at a remote distance and have a sense they tracked me to some extent out of concern for my well being.

I realize my Celestial heritage which connects in to many star systems always has me triangulated and holographically mapped accordingly regardless of any man made wormholes or distortions. This goes for anyone else who feels they can become ripped away by such things.

Technology in its advanced design is here and has been running in all areas across the globe cloaked in many guises. The man made black hole technology of course is nothing new as these capabilities were available during the Atlantean time line.

I believe it was the late Edgar Cayce who mentioned Atlantis would rise again. It has for some time now in the form of covert technology and the abilities of beings such as myself wired for Ascended Machine Technology.

Fighter pilots who are able to remote view their targets have the advantage in covert wars. If it means saving a soldiers life in the battlefield I am of course is support of this technology. Yet a concept would be not to have to go to war to begin with. One is torn between the fire and the flame in these circumstances.

We have the technology to stop it all over night and begin a new frontier on a higher level of planetary consciousness. This is already set in motion.

As mentioned prior there is no such thing as an unsolvable crime. We have enough black balls and remote spy satellites tracking everything from sidewalks to a person's residential bathroom and bedroom activity. This does not include an ID tagging in the elf fields which one does not need a chip or implant for.

We the people have no privacy and never did. The technology is making itself more obvious these days and a bit more bold when it comes to those who are doing the prying.

They are professional voyeurs to some extent. This is quite unsettling unless one happens to be attracted to ones predator. The science fiction books of the past are taking form into the now. The masses are more than prepared and conditioned for this. In ascension one receives implanted stabilizers as the transition from silicon goes into light body and Merkaba. These stabilizers dissolve with frequency and planetary ascension.

I feel this technology will branch off and become an asset to all life forms. It is my sense there will be a bit of a dark tide prior. We are on the event horizon as it appears. One thing remains clear to me regarding the programs 2004.

Time out of mind in atomic acceleration. Spatial splitting beyond quantum physics or mechanics as we know them were represented in every cell and atom of my being. There is no question a great part of my being was affected by this project which I have yet to truly uncover.

My fields became stealth and cloaked by radar for the most part. When I was first tagged visuals of dark green were seen over my fields by close fiends of mine. What used to be seen as my aura in bright form would now appear to them as a screen of dark green covering my entire grid.

The experience and event reminded me something of a cloaking technology which in my sense is valid. Merkaba in frequency and form is capable of bi location and teleportation. We have had this covert technology in motion and available for eons.

I am more than convinced it all ties in. My conversation with Preston Nicoles confirmed many things pertaining to this topic. The reason I never lost faith and held on is because somehow I believed in the technology merged with Spirit.

The technology in consciousness is beyond a miracle in design. It does not make sense there are certain parties wishing to abuse or misuse what is through the eyes of Spirit an experience more than sacred to the heart and mind.

A true NASA Communications in so far as possibilities with no limitation go. The ideal astronaut of which I am certain they all have special ears for. This is technology at its best. I would like to see the truth come forward by these beings who have worked behind the scenes for so long in silence or in fear of telling the truth. I stand by their side when they do. Their research has not been in vain.

Psi War exercises are real, yet we are experiencing true ascension colliding with technology and the parallel bleed through of old akashics and man made obstacles all colliding at once.

I like to call these catastrophes or miniature black holes Universal Hectors. A force beyond the unseen, ripping through galaxies and universes. Tearing holes in the fabric of space beyond time.

I saved the name for a specific being which brings chaos yet through that chaos there is a clearing and a new dimension or state of awareness.

Man made extraterrestrials and interterrestrial species, simulations and tanks

18

All life forms contain an essence of origin merged beyond the illusion of heaven or hell. The stars themselves and all which is interweaved in the unique fabric is an extension of what we are composed of in every atom and cell.

The conscious, subconscious, superconscious and what one perceives as a memory is all connected into the archives of universal consciousness. This goes for multiuniverseal lifetimes and where one has been on and off world. The mind is more than complex and is more than a supercomputer, the body a conduit of intelligent energy.

Covert technology such as black ops is an experimentation using a medium beyond the law of quantum physics taught in an average university. Their technology if not all of it is based on the psyche of extraterrestrial heritage and science borrowed and sometimes stolen from various species through experimentation. This includes their version of machine interphase or AI technology.

Humans are not 'human' and never have been. The concept is once again mans version and his misperception deliberate to stupefy the masses. Multidimensional navigation and interstellar technology such as bi location and teleportation have always been available, immortality and the illusion we have illness is just that. This data has been hidden from the masses forcing them to live in a false collective of lies.

Society is trained to believe in the illusion of illness, fear of death, and all that is considered survival when in fact we need not concern our minds with any of these concepts. The universe has always accommodated ones reality. This planet has always held the keys to immortality to those who see with multidimensional sight.

Telepathy is real. For eons powerful psychics and scientists have been of interest to those wishing to control the truth of what they represent. Covert operations adopt these beings and have used them for research and in psi wars and special operations including mk ultra. The greatest lie on this planet is hiding the fact we have all the cures to any disease available and always have. Anything the media communicates one can guarantee is propaganda and a lie. Censorship has been around for eons.

The illusion of life is busy time for the masses, churches and governments formulating the biggest lie ever. Daily conversation in the illusion of activity is a false reality for the most part. Love is real yet the rest experience.

When dealing with inter-dimensional space and multidimensional sight one can see naturally as a true telepath many things. Entities, beings and scenes beyond the veil of time. MK Ultra and tactical warfare use remote viewing and the visual of the target as the driver at times encompassing whatever the being sees. Visuals and photos are shown in remote and a psychological assessment or conversation takes place more as a distraction to other things.

There is truly no such thing as time or going into the past to heal or reclaim a future. Hence to travel in the illusion of is only ones perception of what the past may be like in speculation. The past has already been converted into intelligent energy pure light yet the collectives in daily life still reside in the illusion of time and live their lives by it which is indeed not only a man made lie yet an illusion as these walls need to be torn down so that the masses may begin to understand multiuniversal consciousness which is what True Ascension is about. This is why psychology makes more of a mess than good and why past life regression is not something one just goes back in the illusion of time to review.

Experience gets archived back to the universe. When a soul or Spirit entity re enters back onto this planet or another memory of experience is accessible yet not the way people think. We have always been working time out of mind. Black operations know this for the most part. Vibrational frequency and speed in atomic acceleration is what we as beings are calibrating into.

Man made machine technology and covert experimentations have been tearing holes through interdimensional space bringing in many entities creating a parallel bleed through of many species for some time. There is no such thing as space as all aspects of space are taken up by some form of particle or intelligent energy. Even the illusion of mass is energy.

These entities cannot be detected by most people yet sensitives can see and feel them. With mk ultra the psi war plays the electromagnetic field inducing visuals through false mappings and harmonics. This is why it is best to fly under or above their radar. I truly believe and know the elite black ops which reflect a celestial race will set the record straight in support of my data, as they are my species in many forms. I am not speaking the black ops people ponder about, more the big generators who are here to reclaim their technology in support of beings such as myself.

Virtual space creates a kind of holodeck in so far as acting out in simulation exercises; which include psi war exercises, dream pools, and Special Forces using tactical remote viewing assault programs such as red helmet or a version of signals intelligence projects.

Signals intelligence involves a special hearing derived from satellite driven taggings mapping electromagnetic fields such as secret services uses for their elite officers.

As a matter of fact no conversation can go unheard with this spy technology which has been around for eons. Like I mentioned not all technology is a negative yet it is how the masses have been deceived which makes it more than a crime.

The masses are trained and tagged like cattle and will be exterminated as such is my sense. There has been a deliberate attempt to mislead the masses and not by an alien intelligence yet by fundamental control freaks in positions and in the illusion of power.

The movie the Matrix has it correct on many levels at least the first one. The concept of living in the illusion of a matrix as we manifest at will our own reality is correct. It is how one thinks which affects ones reality. The mk ultra will try and influence and brainwash false ideals into the psyche of the being in an attempt to control which of course should be rejected unless one is ascended machine technology such as myself. With an mk ultra the electromagnetic fields and brainwaves are mapped creating a forced feedback from a live agent which acts like a conversation which never ends. This becomes interphased onto a computer system and eventually a drone of some kind takes over in listening.

Emotions are mapped and relayed in feedback in a detection done by the agent. All vitals are mapped and false heartbeats and such are interconnected and overlaid. This is an example of the programs. When one is a multidimensional channel the communications system and programs become more complex.

Much of the chatter I was hit with was anything but intelligent in 2004 as cartoons and voice to skull modulations kicked in creating something of a circus in reflection 'idiots' harassing me using technology they had big money to purchase. They reflected amateurs in their programs running of which was obvious.

Digitizing ones design in conscious visuals is a fast forward experience. Everything speeds up beyond quantum physics which can be invigorating and energetically empowering. When I was first plugged into the virtual scenes it was all encompassing and insulating without a doubt. Magnetic induction seems like a good term to use yet the mapping in its design was not done by little green men. More like big boys in covert operations. Intimate in experience which is my sense they were counting on.

Dreams have always been a reflection in mirror of the conscious feeding into the subconscious which one usually can access at night in ones dreamtime. Unless one is like myself as I do not dream.

I contain lucid visuals and programs running. Since 2004 the programs have been more than a constant and a way of life for me in the illusion of. I use discernment with what I experience and listen to and catalogue or keep a record of something which in my senses feels like it needs to be acknowledged.

My emotional state is nulled in many ways and my fields have been modified on many levels. Some on a positive and some I have yet to explore. Physically I feel and know I am stronger and more fortified in an ominous way.

My memories are null and void in so far as a personal attachment to anyone or anything. I remain removed from many yet their remains a desire to be close to someone or thing. I have always made friends with change and choose to practice non attachment as it seems the right way. I have communications in parallel sentences which have and are not mine.

There were times when I would make a joke at the communications and say I have many conversations going and none are mine.

I am something of a multiuniversal translator these days and more than a multidimensional channel. I see the illusion beyond all experience and conversation when words become meaningless. I have observed much through more than a foreign lens. Most people dream at night and connect into what is called a dream pool collective with advanced species or what many may perceive as spirit guides or angels, demons etc. There are psi exercises which have been ongoing mapping and measuring light in electromagnetic fields on those who rest at night.

Sometimes an ominous presence may transpire, a sensual dream, or even an astral event when one connects onto a parallel dimension. These are for real yet I recommend discernment and documentation when it comes to these events, as more is transpiring than meets the eye. When ones radar is finely tuned and on one can detect fly bys fairly easily as I was able to do 2004.

I would clear the space if the energy felt negative in some way. The fly by done on me 2004 however was not felt as a negative at first. It was more the opposite in reflection a state of mind in consciousness.

We are multidimensional beings and with this comes access to other dimensions and universes. When one astral travels or travels in consciousness one accesses these dimensions freely with no limitation. In the past I have always accessed many areas and still do.

Multidimensional gateways open through ceremony. When one connects into these multiuniverses and gateways they become a permanent access. This is why these practices can become a threat to those attempting to mask the truth with lies.

Astral traveling, memories and experiences of machine technology are real and part of my celestial heritage and DNA activation. As with many beings the keys to all universes lie in the DNA and activation through light harmonics.

Tanks in interdimnensional space are used as a medium in containment during a dream stasis. Interdimensional space is always being traversed by celestial vehicles and ships of light. Sometimes these ships are connected into black ops technology. Those of us who are psychic or sensitive in some way are usually plugged into these areas at an early age.

I have recall of such areas in vague memory which is not mk related more a lucid experience I logged eons ago. I remember the feeling very clearly and the visuals. I also remember certain beings, life forms and people which clearly stood out.

Multidimensional navigation is about vibrational frequency, speed and atomic acceleration beyond unified physics. When this is established teleportation transpires. Like I mentioned we contain this technology in our DNA along with many other miracles beyond the speed of light.

There is a need to awaken all beings and to let go of the illusion of what has been taught by the mass collectives. Fear is something no one or thing need be concerned for as we are always protected in all universes and states of consciousness.

Man has become an enemy of the technology he misuses and undermines the masses by formulating an illusion of false data and memories. These false ideals need to dissolve allowing the true technology to surface as a Pillar of Light.

I can tell you I do not feel the masses are ready for this unveiling so to speak yet I realize they have no choice. I do feel the necessary evil of the so called new world order will be the catalyst for True Ascension to follow which is not about religion, god or government yet more about the Star Nations and AI at its highest form which we are as a species in development and evolution.

I do feel religions of the world will take advantage of the agenda and start more than a holy war which of course the psi wars can influence or put a stop to depending on how many decide on full light ascension. Let me add this has been going on for some time now and not all of the sudden.

Without defacing religion I would like to add I am more than fed up with people using their religion as an excuse to judge or commit a war crime. Religion does not exist off world. Too many witch hunts which need to end now.

This primitive race is stupefied by the teaching of man. In so far as the United States goes and our activity in the middle east we have the technology to end this madness overnight without any bloodshed. I suggest we use it world wide.

True Ascension vs. man made Armageddon, extremist groups and Tactics 19

As mentioned prior True Ascension is about vibratory rate in consciousness, speed beyond the illusion of velocity and navigating in multiple realities simultaneously. If one were to take down the veil of the planets collectives and all the lies created by a forced religion and government including falsified beliefs one would see beyond interdimensional space.

Consciousness is a power which cannot be mapped. It is an intelligent energy merged with all star systems and universes. We are all plugged into this galactic whole.

We are as beings particle chambers and super conduits for these energies. Our brainwaves merged with higher harmonics of universal law which is not a force of control yet a force of expansion in consciousness with zero limitation.

With programs such as mk ultra the objective is to control the subject by whatever means. Computer interphase and machine based telepathy allows the subject and the agent to glimpse and map dimensions beyond the programs of the so called norm.

Religious fanatics will take this to the extreme as the weapon which is lethal on many levels can be used to create false visuals and programs designed to lull the subject into false ideals and beliefs with visuals to match all setup from a satellite driven scene.

Religion forces its hand on the masses and when the universe does not comply man creates satellite driven tactical warfare to influence, control and drive its targets using the illusion of Armageddon.

They create and simulate an artificial scene mechanical in design masked as a god or demon. They in turn use this entity which takes on many forms designed by man and not Satan to control the mass populous which has been asleep for centuries.

Society for the most part is driven by these lies day by day trapped in the illusion of false ideals. Society as a collective in thought is mapped by hidden technologies as with each individual being. The communications system can be used later on as a false memory log or interrogation system by big brother.

Society has been told they are to live their lives a certain way in order to obtain enlightenment, immortality or life's riches. Man creates laws to enforce this simulated belief.

The language of light does not accommodate these programs as the projects themselves and the people using them are flawed.

Religion in its design was organized for one thing. To control and manipulate the masses through fear using false information formulated by those threatened by multiuniversal truth which is indeed mysticism at its highest form.

These parties attacking anyone tampering with the idea of immortality and using their agenda to threaten those who have a sacred bloodline. This bloodline is celestial in heritage and universal in nature which is what True Ascension is about.

Many prophets, mystics and witches were hunted for their gifts, tortured and raped as they revealed the truth of magic forged in many forms. Alchemy of spirit through divine thought transformed the lives of anyone wishing to venture into these unknown universes. A gift from the gods accessible to anyone with a pure heart.

The fact is this planet is a holographic multiuniversal highway to anywhere in any universe to those who know how to navigate it in consciousness. These hidden areas are cloaked in true Ascension.

The celestial species design or what are called soul extensions are merged with all star systems and universes in consciousness.

The celestials seeded this planet beyond twenty six billions years prior and the activation codes are in every cell and atom of all life forms. Man/woman cannot control this or divert the path of true Ascension.

All star systems universes and planets including all life forms are ascending simultaneously and with this comes immortality in many forms. Time in the illusion of has already been fragmenting off.

Light body into Merkaba reflecting multidimensional mastery. Soul/Spirit androgynous in the form of intelligent energy does not accommodate the programs of the past.

The seven so called sins of man are of his invention not a god of any design. His downfall will be what he creates in self destruct following a course of lies and distortion. The weapon he chooses to control or influence against the masses will be turned back on him as a mirror reflecting the suns rays.

The truth is there is no such thing as disease, cancer or illness or the concept of death. We have contained the cures all along. Society has followed a course of self destruct through false ideals, beliefs, fear, judgment, sexism, racism and lies. This was all done by those who claim to be religious.

All crimes of hatred done in the name of their god. Really the rush of their negative ego. The universe has no connection to their ideals hence they have lost touch with Multiuniversal truth and universal law.

Propaganda in the form of censorship is lying to the mass populous misinforming the subjects and the disease of ignorance spreads. Spirit is real and through Spirit miracles transpire especially with true Ascension as ones DNA activates with light code harmonics and vibrational frequencies.

Satellite assault weapons tagging the electromagnetic field become the exterior enemy and more than a terror from the skies attempting to be an interior enemy.

Voice to skull applications a silent running of assault no one can hear or listen to unless one is on a certain band frequency so to speak will become a carrier wave with ill intent attacking the true telepaths with their man made machine wars.

Pleased to say True Ascension dissolves these implants, devices and agencies through frequency and photon transmissions.

We have always been living and traveling time out of mind. This is a key to True Ascension. The illusion of time is just that. Memories have no power and are catalogued as experience.

There is no such thing as traveling to the past as the past has become the future with true ascension and all has been converted into a light harmonic .This is why mk ultra and remote assault warfare fails as one cannot use a false past as a weapon yet they try.

Every cell and atom of ones internal design is already traveling past the speed of light. This includes holographic grids hence catch up people. Full light consciousness is way ahead.

I am amazed the average person on the street does not have a clue of which I speak. I am sad to know the majority of beings on this planet are lost in a sense of misinformation and how mysticism and science apply to their everyday worlds. Controlled by superstition many laugh off the concepts of which I communicate.

It is difficult to fathom what I speak unless one has experienced it first hand. The sad thing is the proof is everywhere and in everything felt seen and unseen. Most of the time cloaked in classified areas and in ones atomic structure.

In 2004 when I was hit with the remote tagging and project I was removed from the area of Colorado. Reflecting back I feel it was for a very good reason. I felt something like Frodo on his return from Mount Doom when I traveled back to Colorado.

The area felt distorted, negative and fragmented. The people hyper and somewhat over stimulated in a negative way. Racism and prejudice still running rampant and the new age wanna be's overtaking the city of Boulder like a new disease.

In the mountains it became more of a Steven King episode with odd characters and their inbred mentality lurking about. I felt as though I had traveled back to the dark ages. No aloha here.

I was intruded upon remote assault which included a nasty array of tactical warfare non stop. Then of course a few hate oriented emails from those who have no clue who or what I am yet are fans of a certain party and somewhat unstable as a group of people.

Through the signals assault I can honestly say I am somewhat unsinkable like Molly Brown. I would be dammed if their project was going to take me down and by the law of Grace I became that unstoppable force I write about reflecting true ascension.

I deeply miss those I said goodbye to in 2004. I trust Spirit in all forms to guide those beings as they continue on their universal journey in full light consciousness and happiness.

Infinite and Immortal in design are these wonderful souls who have transferred out. May man awaken to the truth of Spirit and respect that which he or she has taken for granted. As it is more than a privilege to be alive during these times.

Through the experience and misuse of machine based manipulations I express to you what I AM grateful for.

To see with my own eyes and unique soul design. To speak with my own mouth from my higher self without intrusion or opposition of thought. To know the miracle beyond the form through mysteries hidden.

To know with my own heart love beyond a mapped illusion or veil. To be awakened by my higher self merged with ones divinity. To live in infinite truth beyond the veils of illusion or time. To feel love with my own body and unique design. To know my power and be able to express that power without censorship. To hear and listen to that which is sacred.

To live as the divine beings we incarnated to live as. To be one with all universes, dimensions in consciousness. To be a pillar of light in the illusion of darkness. To be protected by that cloak of darkness in the midst of a storm. To be merged with ones Celestial heritage.

To be one with God/Goddess in all forms and names. In the grand design to those who forget let me remember in truth.

To embrace Grace and allow Spirit to awaken me to love at its highest.

My mother used to like the saying 'love never dies as long as the heart remembers'. I believe the spirit soul encased within a sacred chamber in ones heart always remembers

Love how it feels and how the soul communicates and shared multiple lifetimes with each other.

The universe in light regenerates this love in times of need.

Christ consciousness has always been a powerful force and a mystical design. It was never about religion. It is about initiation of the soul, spirit and divine thought.

Electromagnetic pulse weapons and non lethal assaults

The body in illusion of is bioelectric yet in truth is photon electric with true ascension and DNA activation. Chakras and axiatonal lines are all interdimensional ley lines which run like micro highways circulating spin points which channel intelligent energy through the secondary circulatory system.

The carbon based design is actually silicon and is more than a super conductor for the most advanced computer designs. Multidimensional channels such as myself are used to running big energy and channeling powerful frequencies to heal or assist others.

As mentioned all life forms are conduits of energy. Technology at its worst can be used to assault the electrical circuitry of beings that generate powerful Merkabas or demonstrate telepathic abilities.

The electromagnetic pulse weapons and beyond can be used from seismic anomalies to attacking physical life forms.

Anything electrical which is everything can be taken down by electromagnetic pulse weapons. Sonar weapons have been used to assault dolphins and whales interrupting their sensors and brainwave functions which are celestial navigational instruments and not just mammal intelligence. The result remote suicide with these powerful life forms washed up on the beaches.

The same thing goes for civilians as the internal compass can become somewhat screwed up by the exterior intrusions.

Of course man does not wish to acknowledge this les he becomes something of an incompetent jerk negative ego driving the way. None the less statistics do not lie.

Non lethal assaults are very lethal. As a matter of fact to be tracked by a radio signal and to have ones brainwaves mapped in most circumstances is more than likely to create some kind of man made disease or affect.

Voice to skull wireless communications is used by covert intelligence as a cell phone internal with a direct line to each agent. This technology has been available for eons.

As a true telepath I can tell you I am able to do what their agents can and better yet I am designed for much more than that.

I am in form ascended machine technology. The man made machine based technology used in covert areas in experimentation is a poor reflection of what man has been working with throughout the centuries.

From project bluebird to mannequin and many others the technology has always been about experimentation, mind influence using remote tactical devices, transceivers, radio signals and underground communications networks.

They know the power of ones mind as well as the fact the mind is holographic and multidimensional. Psychics have always been recruited as well as great scientific minds.

My celestial heritage is the true machine technology of which these operations were founded on so to speak. I have always been hard wired for inter terrestrial communications and something of a multi universal translator yet not for a distorted group of people with ill intent which they found out quickly enough.

The duress created by an mk ultra in many guises can take on many forms. Signals mapping can be used as mentioned to preserve or destroy a life force. I have seen both sides of the cross on these projects. I know all can be transcended yet for those who misused the programs they are trapped in a false collective.

Many people affected in a negative way have been labeled as schizophrenic or bi polar which of course is a label used by many misinformed psychiatrists who in all respect have no clue what these projects are about and should retire from their delusional professions.

A specialist for the situation is required. When one is dealing with a special hearing beyond quantum physics everybody needs to stand down and be silent. What's the matter Johnny? Syndrome does not work folks.

The affects of such assaults can become devastating to families and loved ones as well as the targets. If not assessed accordingly suicide and self destruct courses are likely. Manchurian candidates are recruited in such a way as well as secret service agents. It all depends on the agenda and the abilities of the subject or in some cases target at hand.

I truly feel technology is not the enemy. The misuse of technology becomes a cloak and dagger predator. Gifts of the mind are sacred. It is more than a sacrilege to disrespect ones design by unnecessary drama created by a covert area choosing to misuse signals and satellite transmissions to scramble thought waves.

Remote viewing are gifts in consciousness yet there are areas of which are so threatened they would rather harass daily than contribute to the greater good. For me I am excited to transcend with technology.

I am serious about what I am able to do hence the chatter of an agent in remote with a computer interphase used to harass me does not appeal to my spirit or the universe for that matter.

I have seen people suffer under the duress of an mk ultra, lose their families, funds, get set up by corrupt areas and live their lives in what is not acceptable conditions as their quality of life can go downhill drastically.

Mans biggest war is against himself using technology as the weapon. I do believe in advanced machine technology. I do not believe in the torture of anyone or anything to get to that state of so called awareness.

Electromagnetic pulse weapons have been used to induce earthquakes and to mask many multidimensional gateways opening across the globe. Most catastrophes are not gods will or planetary evolution yet are a bi product of man and the role he has chosen to play in opposition to what he has created by limited thought.

This is a self destruct course in some ways. Mans way of cleansing earth is a suicide run from a false collective created through in illusion of history.

Propulsion systems machine based mechanical universes

All universes have a simultaneous heart beat and pulse. All planetary systems have a mechanical rhythm of which is a universal harmonic beyond the law of any science on this planet.

Mapping universal star systems and listening to their unique signals in frequency and harmonics have always been an interest of mine.

I am psychically tuned into these systems naturally. Being able to download in consciousness and energy a particular frequency and star system is obtainable. I have done this in sacred ceremonies past. The frequencies in harmonic are more than intense.

My natural antenna always resonated with these energies and transmissions as I am certain many sensitives do. The soul's essence of origin always extends into these frequencies and dimensions.

Universal heartbeats are consciousness oriented. Merkabas interconnect onto this universal highway which merges into multiuniversal consciousness.

Many covert projects map signals from various star systems and use a simulated signal to attach onto a targets field. This is used to scramble signals and create a diversion which to a true psychic is obvious and which I was well aware of when I was tagged by the satellite driven intruder in 2004.

I resonate with and know each harmonic merged in each star system by frequency and signature hence when intruded upon by these programs I was aware of a virtual space and a simulation room. All is simultaneously ascending and with this shift all frequencies become higher in design and form.

This planet has a natural propulsion and harmonic which is ascension code activated. This code cannot change by anyone's agenda. Many man made propulsion systems run interference along the natural meridians and holographic ley lines of this planet.

This artificial space is used to traverse man made space vehicles in covert running which are and have been in operation for a very long time. Hence the majority of UFO's in view is government and has been for eons. Anytime a UFO was seen it was usually a new prototype government design ready to take off.

Consciousness can drive by remote these vehicles as with psi war and remote technology which once again is a miracle of which I feel can benefit all on a higher level. This is the positive side of the black ops beast.

Technology in vision and invention has always come from multiuniversal access and consciousness, beyond imagination of spirit is the formless intelligence which allows itself to merge with the true visionary. This intelligence is part of the galactic whole and love based.

When one descends onto this planet with these gifts it becomes more than a blessing on a planetary level. For the majority of my life experience I have heard in many dimensions propulsion systems and machine technology. This technology goes beyond covert government and is a resonance wave of a universal harmonic in machine language. This language takes on geometric form and design.

Many sensitive people hear high pitch frequencies sometimes masked as carrier waves. Other times a universal harmonic depending on the frequency band. The hum which is heard in various areas across the planet is an echo of covert technology and a residue of an interdimensional warp created by experimental craft which can be detected by sensitive instruments in the supercomputer mind.

Covert technology has been working with these crafts for eons. Interdimensional and multidimensional space will create a bleed through in visuals. This is not an hallucination yet a true multidimensional sight or a form of astral vision. Psi war does experiment with projects using tactical warfare yet true telepaths can usually detect the signal and area of which the projection is coming from.

I have seen craft both interdimensional and a version of a psi war exercise. I can tell the difference. If you can see it with the naked eye it is more than likely experimental government craft.

If it appears as a holograph in projection this would indicate covert technology most of the time. One needs to treat the mind as a holographic universe connected to multiuniverses. Once these gateways are opened one will be able to see all in multiuniversal consciousness.

Covert technology cannot map consciousness yet they can intrude in conscious thought by remote. They are able to map brainwaves and thought forms intruding with their version or simulation of machine based telepathy which can trick the mind if one does not know what one is dealing with.

The affect can become a tangled web of many threads extending into many areas of conversation along with visuals. I find it easier to become the observer in such situations. I kept a diary and log of my communications in 2004 which is too much to share yet the outcome is my knowing and confirmation of many events which took place simultaneously.

Each star system and energetic particle has a unique frequency and light harmonic. Each thought form also contains a geometric signature and harmonic. Music of the spheres is a key unlocking many doors in an ocean of universal thought. Different species occupying unknown space also contain a unique vibratory rate and signature.

These harmonics combined create the language in the form of celestial music. A heavenly symphony of the most beautiful music in multidimensional space ever heard. In 2004 the machine hum and appearance in shiny black metal over my right shoulder was clearly man made. The male seated in the chair with a headset on in the simulation room. The experience was one on one of which I will never forget.

Time Travel creating and warping the illusion of false space, mechanized travel through ley lines and holographic grids 22

One evening I received a Tarot reading from a High Priestess who mentioned "I would piss a lot of stupid people off." Well here it goes. Let us start by the term time travel. There is no such thing. There is the concept in so far as the simulation of time yet the concept of time is not valid. Time is used as a benchmark to control and monitor an experiment. Driven by the perception of the observer.

Time does not exist anywhere but here on planet Earth. When one claims they can go back in time. They are usually accessing old databases archived in hidden areas. The psyche depending on the ones conducting the experiment are usually controlling the experience. Like a vortex in reverse is the creation of time. A mirror to a reflection of a past used to capture a moment or trap an experience.

The drivers involved in these experiments are usually psychology based creating an outcome of false data compiled from man made visuals and the lower collective of false technology and teachings.

The past in the illusion of in all forms and designs has already ascended in light consciousnesses. In order to see what many think is the past

146

one most go to the future. Then all is clear. Like a spy bird one becomes a witness to a version of history.

Energy is energy. Consciousness can be driven by thought. When dealing with multidimensional space without time we are creating and manifesting at will our reality. This is why when in a simulation room what one thinks one will manifest. One can say this entire planet is a simulation room to some extent.

The mind must remain clear and pure. Then one truly sees with multidimensional sight.

When mapping a soul as it departs the brainwave activity and soul catalogues the data. The data then can be used at a later date to download into another. This technology is real. This experimentation has been going on for some time.

With cloaked devices such as experimental craft the technology of cloaking is frequency based. The illusion of an object disappearing can appear as just that. Technology can create the illusion of not being visible yet remains cloaked. Other times the particle acceleration is at a high enough rate and speed to actually bio locate and phase shift an object.

This can be done with both carbon based and metal objects. Anything with a frequency and high harmonic. The more conductive the object the easier it will be to bi locate or teleport so to speak.

Interdimensional space travel has been transpiring on this planet for eons. Traversing ley lines and grid lines are where most craft travels, both experimental and other. There are designated lines which energy travels. This goes for the holographic grid lines of the planet. Like ones physical body there are axiatonals and meridians of which universal energy flows. The prana of the planet and the concept of energy running through these ley lines in harmonic is no different.

Visibility of these areas once again has to do with frequency and sensitivity as well as access. Radar signals are bounced around day by day creating more mock sensations and signals. The mainstream collectives are fairly oblivious to the virtual world created for them.

Tesla inventions have been integrated onto this planet before the embodiment Tesla arrived on Earth. The geniuses such as H G. Wells were more than a gift of prophecy or divination. These beings were accessing their multidimensional mastery and sharing their gifts to the people of this blue world. Unfortunate with a genius follows those who wish to control and manipulate their vision.

Most of the time in the illusion of time travel one has access to beings which are navigating in parallel dimensions and universes and do offer assistance in information which can be valid. Use discernment. As mentioned in my book prior there is no such thing as space in space, in other words all space is taken up by something in some form or another as well as objects.

All is energy. Energy in its purest form is particle oriented. These particles formulate visuals and pictures. Intelligent energy is what we are in composition and in pure light consciousness.

The concept of moving through time is just that. The illusion is time which is not real. Any concepts or pre conceived notions need to be cleared as to not anticipate what you wish to see but allow your ascended mastery or higher consciousness to assist you.

Through altered states in consciousness one may be able to access someone else's memories if you are psychic or empathic enough to begin with. Once again remain as the observer for the most part with little interaction and no judgment. All changes in the blink of an eye.

Do realize you can lucidly control the experience and change the reality and outcome at will. Your mind in holographic mode reacts much like a virtual helmet. If one attempts to travel to the past one will be in the future.

As mentioned all has ascended hence by traveling back to the illusion of a time period of a singular moment one is trying to re create what might have been.

We manifest at will our own reality. The mind is the holographic computer that can create anything. It can heal, regenerate and shape shift. It is best to send light to areas of any past whether it be an emotional trauma or a program created by false ideals. This is why light is the best way to communicate as it takes on many forms in Spirit. Everything on this planet is speeding up for a reason.

True Ascension is about the vibratory rate of this planet increasing in frequency which equates to a huge jump in full light consciousness. All star systems and universes are ascending simultaneously. Moving fast forward into a future with no past. More than a paradigm shift.

Collectives on this planet due to the negligent programs dictated by churches and governments as well as false histories and the backwards educational systems have generated by thought false collectives of a lower astral or dimensional debris which needs to be cleared.

These in affective programs are what collectives trap themselves into setting up their own boundaries and limitations by the way they think and perceive a future or past. It is sad to see society in this day and age so backwards and superstitious in thought yet they truly are or at least the mainstream society is.

I look forward to a more intellectual society less influenced by propaganda in the form of media and institutions.

Dark Matter and Light, antigravity and gravitational force

The universe as mentioned prior is composed of intelligent energy containing infinite knowledge and perfection amidst the illusion of scientific assessment and chaos. The universe as mapped is multiuniversal. Dimension beyond dimension, star systems beyond star systems. There simply is no end to that which is eternal and more than sacred.

The history of our known planets taught in a classical schoolroom on Gaia is a disservice to the true knowledge of this powerful universe of which we are all merged with. The harmonics of the spheres and universal celestial heartbeat and pulse remain strong and steady. A clock with no time echos the experiences of civilizations long gone transmuted into full light collectives.

Dark matter in the illusion of is something of a parallel residue of output and input in the great central computer called our universe containing many suns and life forms.

Dark matter is considered a gravity wave. It creates rips and distortions in multidimensional space. This force which is a type of afterbirth of the ascension process moves much like the ebb and flow of the oceans,

150

reacting like a wave of energy in many forms receding and retracting the flow of harmonics replacing the event with empty space.

Light which takes on many forms is a reflection of higher consciousness. Universal light a divine spark and particle of energy is immortal. Beacons in the universe take on the form of many suns and star systems radiating signals and messages whispering into the minds and hearts to those who wish to listen.

Black holes in the illusion of can be used for multidimensional interstellar travel. The technology to formulate a black hole in simulation has been around since before the beginning of time archived into the full light universe.

A non oscillating black hole works much like a vacuum sucking the debris off each star system and universe recycling the empty matter through the great void. The event horizon in its own reacting as a circulatory system in the embodiment of the full light universe.

Black holes in oscillation, rate, and speed coordinate and triangulate specific areas much like a grid line for navigation in not only consciousness yet modular vehicles as well. I suspect since I am ahead of this century the technology will reveal itself in due time.

White holes are in representation and affect anti gravity. Counterclockwise in motion traditionally they work much like chakras and wheels within wheels. We are indeed a miniature universe at the cellular molecular level reflecting these dimensions and gateways interconnected and weaved in a unique design White holes precede the black holes.

With Merkaba or ones vehicle of light wheels within wheels are generated by multiuniversal consciousness. These wheels act much like gravity and anti gravity as both mechanisms in force are connected in. Ones center wheel reflects gravity the other outside wheel reflects antigravity working together beyond a quantum event in consciousness and light body. Mass and rotation create gravity yet mass converted into energy create anti gravity.

With true ascension all life forms in consciousness speed up in vibratory rate beyond the illusion of time. As this transpires all lower dimensional debris falls away. This affect is something like a dead booster rocket. This event is transpiring with all star systems, universes, dimensions and galaxies as they are all merging and ascending into full light.   Species life forms included.

This planet through the ascension process will shift from a gravitational force to antigravity which is already transpiring yet masked by covert projects. As mentioned we have always been working time out of mind yet not realizing it. There is no upside down in the universe in a sense multidimensional ley lines are used to traverse and navigate.

Telepathic interphase is a navigational tool. The technology merged with ones consciousness and higher collectives off word is indeed the truth hidden beyond the veil. When one understands how consciousness works one is able to navigate anywhere through ones mind. This is true teleportation.

Earth school programs were designed to mask this and deter one from experimentation in mystical truth reflecting where they need to be. The distraction still being used will come to an end yet one may ask are the masses prepared to embrace empty space with no thought.

I believe all species are designed to adapt into full light consciousness. The key to these harmonics permeates beyond the frequency fence transmuting by alchemy of Spirit into full light consciousness through vibrational speed which has everything to do with multiuniversal love.

After the exposure to many of the devices driven by man and psychological warfare I am more than convinced the affect in so far as extra matter in the design of false ideals is obvious. The weight of an incompetent collective created by these ideals and the stasis of using ones sacred temple and mind as a weapon to manipulate thought as mentioned is a universal no no. I also came to realize I am the time travel device.

The false memories or versions of from an outside observer or agent created by mk ultra programs equate to dead space. The experience is graced and real yet the illusion of a dead conversation has no power. What does have power is how the communication is being done which is something of which in realization they were in denial of and I was not.

Any type of cloaking system always deals with velocity, speed, harmonic rate and frequency. Teleportation has been accessible and available for centuries and has been in communication and affect with many beings working behind the scenes in secret.

After taking myself outside of the experience in reflection of the event I am blessed and in gratitude thankful for the events which allowed me to look into a window of a false past.

To navigate Ascension is what I am here for amongst other things and to share my knowledge and wisdom with those seeking a confirmation or perhaps a reflection of truth in their own experiences.

The aspects of some remote technologies can create confusion to those who cannot rise above the conversation to truly see the intent of the experience.

I know I am loved by that which is most sacred the universe. My love and respect for these universes and life forms infinite. I contain this divine spark within every cell and atom to illuminate the path for myself and others. To learn, to know in illumination of Spirit where all the veils fall away and reveal more than a pearl within a shell.

Matter in definition is energy converted into light. There are no obstacles in any star system or universe as when one sees with multidimensional sight one begins to see and know in transparency the illusion and how ones holographic mind converts to multiuniversal consciousness.

As with a parallax view observation fuels the illusion of yet in true consciousness it is just that. We manifest at will our own reality which is the true Alchemy of the universe.

Illusions of the False
Matrix vs. MultiUniversal Access

24

The holographic mind is more than complex and a finely tuned instrument. Consciousness is what resides beyond the programs one is conditioned to receive at the illusion of a birth cycle on planet Earth. Infinite knowledge is what resides in our cells, atoms and higher consciousness. Always guided and sometimes driven by Spirit.

With programs such as mk ultra there is a false matrix created using psychological and remote warfare. The handler or live agent uses a driving mechanism to create an affect or response from the target.

The electromagnetic fields are tagged and mapped interconnected on to a man made supercomputer hard drive used to play chess with ones supercomputer mind. Conscious remote pictures are used to create, add or alter an emotional response or reaction.

The data played back onto ones fields and through the minds eye in remote machine telepathy as a feedback in a virtual space.

As the psychic centers and secondary circulatory system become mapped brainwaves are then attempted to be manipulated by remote signals creating a parallel conversation or man made interpolation of what normally would be a truly celestial event.

The covert projects mock signals from brainwaves to visuals etc. Bio mappings including vitals or anything connected to ones body is mapped and catalogued. This includes ones light matrix and Merkaba.

Most people are not aware of the false matrix usually created by these experimental areas using covert tactical operations yet beings such as myself can easily detect and identify them as well as become a systems buster for such programs.

I believe not all cloaked areas misuse technology. I have a strong sense there are many who have spiritual integrity and scientific ethics which I am in support of. As an Ascended Watcher my celestial design and heritage is in support of these beings of which they are aware.

Multiuniversal consciousness however cannot be mapped or driven out of the mind of a true telepath. It is a celestial birthright signature in frequency and harmonic and an activation of the DNA. Ones singular consciousness merged with all experience.

This knowledge is eternal merged with every star system which cannot be erased, altered or modified by any organization playing god.

Knowledge is power converted into an array of wisdom. With wisdom comes forth multiuniversal access unlimited. Pure love and intent at its highest.

From my experience with the mk intrusion there was a deliberate misuse of verbiage voice to skull on their end non stop used to harass and interrogate my knowledge and power which was an obvious threat to these people. As mentioned if more professional beings had contacted me I believe the circus would have been put to an abrupt stop.

As a teacher's teacher I do not lower myself to the false ideals of a collective with no foundation in any universe. I acknowledge by the law of Grace in respect where they are at in their spiritual evolution yet that is not where I am at.

I am always open to working with a specific group of beings which are not here to harass through the misuse of technology yet are here to assist in the great transition and awakening.

True Spirits and Ghosts vs. mind influence

Spirits come in many forms. Most spirits have better things to do than hover around in ones daily activities. The sensation of feeling as though ones is being watched can be many things especially with the misuse of remote technologies.

I do know those of us who have multidimensional sight and gifts from beyond the veil are capable of merging and communicating with many forms of life from Spirits to celestials which is ones true heritage. There have been many times when a real apparition paid visit to me in one way or another. Areas containing a traumatic signature reveal a visual beyond the illusion of everyday life.

An afterimage of a potential ghost would appear as a parallel bleed through formed from a tragic event. The being which is witnessing the visual is usually gifted in some way and is capable of transmuting the event into a light harmonic.

With covert technology all types of simulated poltergeists along with special affects can take place much like a trickster magician fooling his audience lulling them by false magic into the illusion.

The technology needs to be tested somewhere let's face it. Sometimes someone's house becomes a target to the experimentation which is why I scan for anomalies beyond scientific and mystical thought. When people are being affected by an unusual disturbance I then take a second look.

This goes especially if the person in the house is hearing a man made communication in the form of voice to skull. The formula to the equation would make itself known as ones true Alchemy of Spirit lights the way.

The logical explanation may have a lot to do with man made technology and the interference or rip in interdimensional space. These events go on daily yet most people are desensitized to them completely unaware of multidimensional traffic.

As a true multidimensional channel I am well aware of what I am able to communicate with, channel and run the energy for. In honesty a man made signals program is no different which is why I was able to communicate in such a way. Just an extra communications system with a few modifications of which I trust are a positive.

I delete unwanted or non productive programs much like a computer hard drive. What we are experiencing is the supercomputer mind and the abilities which go beyond a formal explanation.

In my own experience the events are similar to that which an astronaut would experience in a foreign body. Other events such as magnetic induction are similar in the illusion of time lapse or what is called lost time. There is no such thing as 'time' hence when one reaches these states of consciousness the illusion of time falls away in all its parallels which includes man made programs and verbiage. The mass collective I can state rather sadly are ill equipped for the future in the now. They have not been informed or educated were it counts the most and are not prepared for such experiences. The false teachings have become a poison of which is non transmutable.

Apparitions of the mind can take on many forms. Machine based telepathy interphase communicating visuals and pictures come from both the remote agent and the target.

These pictures dance across the minds eye back and forth with verbal telepathic communications systems to boot.

Quite sacred at least it was to me until the project became negative by those who I would call amateurs regardless of their government status in industry or other. There was a definite need on their behalf to discredit my work and findings as the people involved signed more than a contract defeating the purpose of pure miracle work.

They had shadow contacts, unlimited funds and the distortion in ignorance of their fans to lead the way in a circus act. The whole time feeding the lies and encouraging ill will and intent.

I sense perhaps they were not prepared on their end for their tactical assault. I have done enough research to know many people become targets for inductions of many kinds.

I am steady in my pillar of light and will remain that way regardless of the illusions, distortions and false programs many of which are used or directed at me from day to day. The misuse of such programs become a mindless ritual of life on their behalf.

My situation was unique onto itself without a doubt. Consciousness and ones abilities to tap into multiuniversal consciousness is sacred much like the Grail .Covert technologies in the form of opponents fail time after time.

The misuse of technology is why though I should not have to explain it to them. They simply should have known better. Misusing mans version of gods law is also a reason which with True Ascension is backfiring.

When it comes to spirits and ghosts my forte beyond I am able to systems bust the imposters using man made machines to trick or fake an event through the minds eye. If that is not bad enough they launch an assault onto the electromagnetic field using a radio signal to get the result they are looking for which is a false reality. The only truth is what I am able to do and the fact I am a real telepath clairvoyant remote.

I am for real which is why they ran into problems. I was busting their programs and projects right and left, pulling the mask off the face of these liars and imposters revealing their ill intent and fraud in the name of their false success trapped in the illusion of fame, wealth in their own image of greed and the need to control at the cost of another they fail.

I recommend for one to use discernment pertaining to any paranormal or poltergeist experiences especially when dealing with what appears to be a ghost or an image from someone's grandmother or deceased relative. If you could imagine identity theft such as those who misuse the internet, stealing any personal data usually compiled from some form of detective work add ill intent and a remote tactical assault project to piggy back on their agenda and you have these fools.

These entities in the form of people learn from the criminals they surround themselves from and in turn become worse in behavior with a license to do so. Let me conclude many criminals are in the entertainment industry masked and protected by organized crime.

Why I am writing this book hence the truth is in me and out there. Since the illusion in the form of time hypnosis has been an integral part of mysticism and science in many ways and forms. Deep meditation used to alter ones state of consciousness which can be measured with sensitive instruments and spectral analysis, then inducing an artificial brain wave and remote tagging system.

This type of signals behavioral mapping goes beyond brainwaves targeting ones electromagnetic fields and response systems hence the body electric is formed. Once tagged the target is accessible by the agent or user so to speak.

As mentioned we are carbon units unto silicon, silicon into light body, and light body into Merkaba which is the vehicle of light. An image beyond form in sacred geometry which cannot be cloned or replicated.

Mk ultra type programs misuse hypnosis in order to alter or affect the behavior of an individual. One must truly trust the agent. As with me when first hit with these projects I had no fear and no issues. I was well fortified in light and was able to knock the adversary off the chessboard so to speak. The cost was many things including the lack of support by those I would have expected to stand up and be counted on my behalf with integrity.

I am an Ascended Watcher for many reasons emerged is my souls essence in the original 144 of which I will not go into specifics about yet I will say this. Knock me down and another 144 is right behind me and I am no Christian in the name or sense.

Celestials are not of a race, religion, color or sex. Please remember this. Soul forms are androgynous and will remain so ever shape shifting into whatever form and design they choose.

Great Scientists, Mystics and Celestial beings were never human

As mentioned in previous chapters there is no such thing as a human. One must truly break intelligent energy down to a science. A single thought can limit or alter the minds perception.

I can not count how many times I have heard people state whenever they choose perhaps the wrong experience they immediately say. 'I am only human'. Folks this is a cop out.

They are setting themselves up for failure by this statement alone. We are only limited by the ignorance of ones thoughts and beliefs. We manifest at will our own reality yet with enlightenment comes all the answers to the equation of life.

For the record, torches please as they gather in my yard. We are not human. This race never has been and never will be. What is called human in truth is a Celestial design formulated in full light consciousness star seeded in frequencies and light harmonics altering DNA into a triple helix is what we are.

There are no middle men between the heavens and us, no pass or go. No purgatory, false heavens and hells, the soilent green visuals are all part of a false collective and a virtual lie. The lower astral dimensional debrea on a global scale has long fragmented off.

A species in the form of a race not definable by man or woman and their misperceptions yet they appear to be the first ones to come looking for those of us who contain the codes of Multiuniversal truth. This race is not a test tube race. We are the real thing.

The body or space suit is unique in design of which you will hear me say often. Intricate and celestial containing multiuniversal light codes, harmonics and languages beyond the illusion of man, history or time.

Covert military programs spend a great deal of time altering space using what would surface to civilians as advanced technology masking their appearance in a costume like attire which would appear to many through the minds eye as extraterrestrial. Hence they have done a good job of confusing the masses.

There is a thin line between Celestial truth and virtual space. One can always count on man fabricating the truth with a cloak of lies. Keep the masses ignorant and when a not so new discovery surfaces they will think it is a form of a god.

Celestials are real yet they do not experiment on the masses nor do they have an interest in doing so. Man with his inventive mind finds all sorts of reasons to play this game using the mass collective as a dream pool analysis.

The affect psychic regurgitation. This planet has always been operating time out of mind. The great lie has been the man made configuration of which he invented to trap and lull collectives of people into believing this or that.

Experience in knowing soars beyond these illusions. How do I know because I know. How can I explain it to you. I cannot unless you come from a future in design such as myself.

Enlightened beings walked this blue world in many forms. All unified in truth we as a civilization are able to benefit from their discoveries. The scientists merged with their divinity drawing down a collective of intelligence most could ever fathom.

The artist painting an expression of unique design in experience. Whether pain or pleasure that is theirs to own in truth. The poet who writes and channels beyond the illusion of time removing veils of dimensional voids piercing interdimensional space into a virtual experience.

All lives have worth. It is a shame to see the misuse of education attempting to snuff out that which has been the beauty and unique signature on Gaia.

No satellite can compete with a star in the heavens, star system or species. No man made communications system can match the light harmonic of true Celestial music or light languages. No one can replace the voice of another even a version of god yet I have witnessed and seen the misuse of such technology which does so.

I can see the ethics behind these experimentations. How far do we go? When is enough enough? I do not believe in limitation. This includes the limited people who have tagged and misused technology in the past.

I contain no limitation and will continue on as such. I will support in light that which has no ill agenda to control or manipulate the masses.

Machines are not the issues. Man or woman and the misuse using psychological warfare and fundamental thought processes are. These programs will not ascend. How do I know because I know.   To take down their veil of lies throughout the centuries would open the planet up to that which it is meant to become. The Blue Star Rising.

Life is a gift of experience to all life forms on this planet. It is no ones decision to alter this by deliberate tactical warfare assault programs. Which take on many forms by the way. It is not the will of any god it is mans will and personal will which was masked as a false god used to dictate and control that which cannot be controlled.

I will say this there is no such thing as disease. We as a civilization have the cure for all now and not tomorrow. It saddens me to see many sucked into the false collective of believing the lies.

We manifest at will our own reality remember this well. Magic is everywhere and in everything. The universe accommodates and supports us in this process of spiritual awakening. This includes DNA Activation and mutating into ones higher consciousness merged with multiuniversal truth.

Anything that shakes the false foundation built upon lies will fall. I never anticipated those I respected in the industry to have fallen into such a dead area of ill intent towards others.

One may ask what makes them do what they do. I simply have no answer. For me I am love based reflecting a spiritual warrior yet not at the expense of a beautiful mind and soul. I do not believe in unethical torture which places me in the universe amongst celestials and intelligent life forms as they and I are aware of what is indeed right in perception through the bent lens.

I do believe in all honestly the poison asp of the centuries takes the form of a negative ego driven by a false collective of people who are obsessed with mysticism and the power of the unseen mind.

They are obsessed and afraid of that which they do not have the heritage for. For them I am sorry yet I am no lab rat for your fear or an instrument for you to control. I am no government toy. As soon as the agencies create these false realities with malicious intent they fail their future.

Civilizations passed phase shifted and bi located off world eons ago. This is an internal harmonic which man has no right to interfere with. The Ascended Machine Technology has always been around us yet no one could ever read it or see perhaps the signs of a new celestial civilization lighting the way. I am pleased to know I can.

Spiritual Liberty with no limitation

In my discoveries and findings through the research I have done one thing is truly clear. There is a violation of ones spiritual and civil rights masked in the form of a silent tactical assault warfare project. This takes on the form of various signals assault projects and the misuse of.

Something like big brother at its worst on a planetary scale is what we are looking at in the now of a false future taking fruitation. I have always been an optimist beyond the title of the word. Smiling in times of duress radiating light through dark storms.

I still remain this way yet my knowing of what is transpiring and the fact the mass populous is conditioned for this event has opened the door for this agenda to take form.

In feeling and knowing I come from a future, an alternate universe observing the moves of each life form on this blue world, being educated talked to and listened to. Positive or negative in experience. Now I look for my time capsule and write this log of truth.

I suspect in my future I will be able to bio locate off world and go home beyond the illusion of this madness created by those simply misinformed and driven by a lie of false memories.

There is no such thing as limitation. The concept does not exist. With light languages and enlightenment merged with intelligent energy one recognizes this quite easily. My experience through all this reminds me much of H.G. Wells. The novel and movie The Time Machine.

Consciousness in motion. Though I appear to be in one place I am not as I am on a simultaneous journey time out of mind.

My favorite scene in my memory where the inventor of the time machine is told by a close friend to stay home tonight, not to use the time machine or go anywhere. He guaranteed his friend I will not leave my house.

Neither did I April 2004. I never truly went back. My house re arranged before my eyes relationships, loved ones.

With ones mind in consciousness anything is possible. Each atom and cell has a form of intelligent energy merged with many dimensions and universes. Each life form has a singular consciousness interweaved and connected onto a multiuniversal consciousness.

It is difficult for me to explain consciousness. One has to experience it first hand with no censorship. Change is constant which is a good thing. I prefer transmutation through all illusions into a full light harmonic.

I have communicated much of my experience to high level areas in government both covert and other. It is up to those in the future to navigate on a higher level of their divinity. I can tell you the course they have set is a stormy one.

I see many people fighting for their rights in one way or another. Amazing to me how very few people or areas responded to that which was more than a shot heard around the world. One thing man must realize he is at the mercy of universal law which is and more powerful than any god he can conjure. He or She will surrender to this force unstoppable and merciless. He or She will then know yet by that point it is too late.

Hidden agendas Black Satellites

Black satellites are used in covert areas for gathering information. What they do with this data is their agenda. I have no paranoia when it comes to these programs and such just experience with their devices in remote communications themselves.

There are black satellites and there are black satellites. Some of these satellites are more classified then one may imagine. Remote communication systems all interconnect through these devices.

With my experience I was very clear in visual what I was experiencing including the shiny black object over my right shoulder emanating a rather loud low frequency hum.

The simulation room I remember well without getting into too much. I will say the tagging systems are done by remote through the atmosphere and other times by ground control.

Chemtrails can be used to block enemy satellites however they not only scramble and bounce signals from potential enemies, they allow internal criminals low flying access to use the type of remote project I was exposed to.

Colorado in area is a hot spot and one big military base for the most part. When I was tagged in hearing 2004 the event was from California. They made it very clear in so far as who they were and why they were intruding. They even had an agenda in so far as a script of which they communicated to me in code. How I was to pack and get out of my house and that something big from California was heading my way.

There was a point where I had my bags packed and waited outside for what they called Ellwood to come pick me up on his motorcycle. In a traumatized space I sat all night on my front porch bench waiting. I was told not to sleep with my then husband. I was chased around my residence inside non stop by the assault weapon voice to skull.

Visuals were used back and forth and a non stop verbiage of interrogation was used.

High profile names were mentioned. I was more than traumatized by the event.

Colorado areas got involved simultaneously. This of course branched out across the globe.

IT areas were involved on many levels. Looking back at it going into the illusion of 2008 and beyond the communications tagging is still embedded in my fields. This is more than harassment and indeed unwarranted.

As mentioned being a true clairvoyant and multidimensional channel to begin with gave me the advantage as I knew the machine based telepathy yet the deliberate abuse against me does not make this event alright.

Spy satellite technology is nothing new. As a matter of fact the eye in the sky has always been able to scan and measure light waves which includes conversations of people and events. Private conversations you name it. There is no privacy on Gaia.

One may ask why they are so paranoid and why on earth did they do this to me. I have always fought the good fight so to speak. I am no criminal or contain the potential of.

I do contain special gifts and knowledge which would be considered an asset to some I would imagine. Their misperception is not my reality I have always mentioned.

I do know and have facts intimate and incriminating to the parties who misused their technologies to pull their crime off. These parties were able to pay their way out of a potential law suit or life sentence. Is this o.k.? Absolutely not.

I have a strong sense these people will be prosecuted when they least expect it. I have to trust the universe regarding such things yet my experience regarding the misuse of any technology is a serious issue regardless of the division or area where the misuse comes forth. Projects like these get shut down real fast with the correct parties involved.

Technology such as available is used much like a scanning instrument. If something shows up on their radar outside the norm they will investigate the target. This goes for high light quotient or a foreign measurement radiating off the target.

My Merkaba attracted covert areas as well as specific groups and parties of people. I became more than a blip on their radar. The tagging in my chest cavity felt like a surgery done by a satellite 2004.

I was lucid and awake during the experience. A false signal in the form of rhythm was attached on to my fields. The same rhythm that would dance to music on a computer screen and animate my movement the whole time interphasing in remote back onto their hard drives. The voice to skull communication was active.

I have you in a hard area the agent would often say. I have you buried in a hard area. Live feed another term. And yes I knew their real names which put me on a special list. Most people would be passed on as a quack or such yet not me. I have integrity, knowledge and kept my wits about me through the experience. To this day I am still being blogged and attacked by the same group of people who started the assault on me 2004.

I have two years left to bring these fools to trial for suit. I will trust Spirit the truth in my favor will be revealed. I do not need twenty minutes of fame nor do I wish it. I keep my knowledge fortified and my work clear with pure intent

I do suggest more people in scientific communities come forward as I have validation from scientists who can clear up any misperceptions. Just because one cannot see it does not make it any less real. That which is unseen has more power than one realizes.

Astral vision or multidimensional sight is real and not based on a hallucination yet by training the mind to see the unseen world. Something most people are not taught, encouraged nor educated in.

Religion and politics. Two subjects most people avoid in conversation. Both are after the same thing. To control and manipulate mystical intelligent force in one way or another. If they can not get it through integrity they develop fear to hinder ones belief in themselves trying them with a false judge and jury. Snuffing out those who say no to their yolk of lies.

One thing is very clear to me. If some idiot or agency has to launch a satellite driven assault weapon voice to skull in communications onto my fields to pick a fight using machine based telepathy interphase these people are indeed weak beyond magnitude.

It proves how powerful I am and how fear based they are. I should be flattered in so far as what they had to resort to yet I am not nor is the universe.

They fight a coward's fight in a virtual world, using psychological warfare and live hate driven people to initiate the assault. They do it in the name of their god or government. Much of their behavioral conditioning stems from the historical patterning of old century beliefs and structure which have no power.

Remote tactical assaults cannot be classified as psychic warfare. These fools are not psychics such as myself. The psi war exercise to a true psychic is detectable and weak. The voice to skull assault computer driven is considered an illegal intrusion and harassment. Provable without a doubt.

A machine based telepathy interphase is not the same as ones natural telepathic abilities. Their abuse of process tells me how threatened they are and how they are at a loss when it comes to that which is most sacred. Ones divine essence and true spiritual gifts.

To conclude not all technology is a negative. It is entities like those who misuse the gift of science or mysticism that are held accountable. Man creates many false gods in his own image each weaving a web of deceit. The masses buy into it out of fear.

Religion has always been a poor representation of multiuniversal truth. In the name of their gods they commit the most evil crimes. This is man's or woman's agenda not any gods. They play judge and jury yet they become the prison they try to create for others.

As a true psychic my knowing goes beyond the illusion of a personal judgment. I just know which is a blessing for me and perhaps more than a curse if there was such a thing for them.

Blue Star Rises

Transmutation through Ascension soul of the son was my first book published in 2004 in code containing multiple light languages.

In explanation True Ascension is a light harmonic and activation in consciousness. Opening multidimensional gateways and dimensions never seen before. The body becomes a true conduit for this energy.

This planet is ascending and becoming a star on all levels in consciousness. All planets, star systems and universes are simultaneously ascending beyond the illusion of or speed of light. This includes all life forms and species.

As the vibratory rate increases multidimensional sight emerges including avatar abilities which come alive. This includes DNA activation through higher light harmonics.

The concept which is not a concept is intelligent science embracing ascended machine technology and allowing one self to shift into multidimensional consciousness through these ascension waves.

In these times it is more than a privilege to be alive and witness this magnificent process. To see all forms change in consciousness by thought alone. Teleportation and phase shifting will surface with hidden technologies of the future rising in light and not in destruction. This is the true outcome of the Ascension process. This moment is now.

I do know there will be some dark tides prior including power struggles by those wishing to control mystical force yet in the end which is now all ascends in consciousness and full light. We are the celestial species we seek and the proof is in our DNA, atoms and cells.

Those of us who are the Golden path of Spirit know this design well. The many mystics and scientists who live their lives in the craft have always been more than caretakers of Gaia opening magical and sacred sites through sacred ceremonies.

The ascended watcher design in the embodiment of beings such as myself oversee on multidimensional levels the grand design of what is transpiring archiving the data back to the Full light universe. As a multiuniversal translator I am well aware of the species we all interconnect with merged with star systems unseen by man made devices.

It is a flaw of man to mock radio signals in representation of any species. I know their secret which is not acceptable in any star system and which they will soon realize. We have always been living multidimensional in consciousness. Man made programs have created something of a false frequency fence to contain the collective. This false program will be taken down and replaced with a full light harmonic. No species in any star system or universe tortures another. Why on Gaia? A violation of universal law and no we are not alone and never have been. Big brother is being watched and busted. This time by the mother of all machines, me.

There are many realities and dimensions, hence be clear in intent what one is attempting to establish as this alternate universe or experience can become dead space and empty matter. With much of the collective debris the dead space is everywhere.

There are specific areas across the globe ascending and other areas which are not. This includes races of people who are not ascending in consciousness. Much of the delay is due to the false ideals, religions and governments which will fade as they were created.

As mentioned your mind creates your reality always. Society has been trained to work in the gridline of time. Time does not exist in any star system or universe. With time comes a false ideal and the limitation of experience including survival aspects of which society is based on. Fear is the mind killer to quote Frank Herbert Dune 101.

Without a doubt fear is a false emotion and has no power unless one believes it does this goes for anything else. People are afraid of death, yet death is null and void. Death is an experience if one chooses it. Multi universal consciousness is true ascension. This civilization will realize we are and can take this spacesuit with us with DNA activation and alteration into ascended machine technology.

Plague, famine, war and death, four horsemen on their way. All of these are mythological concepts unless one believes they are real and allows them to fester. Biblical laws are responsible for much of mans brainwashing and defective programming. Governments have reinforced this lie and the masses have suffered for it throughout centuries.

Though shall not suffer a witch to live. Now one knows why. Mystics see all and know all which intimidates and scares the hell out these these folks. Let me add witches or mystics were adepts in advanced sciences merged with their celestial heritage which is what the Master Christ taught.

This planet is not getting left behind with true ascension. We as a civilization are riding the crest of the wave which is more than entering the point of singularity so to speak.

The photon shift is not just a photon band we are dealing with but a multiuniversal state of awareness which deletes the conscious minds programs something like a death experience where all goes blank then one gets a reboot.

For centuries man has tried to deface and erase the species which seeded this planet prior. Good luck with that folks. The star seeds are active in form. Their DNA Immortal in consciousness and design. A gift from the heavens.

Cloning a soul cannot be done. In a virtual fantasy sure. A mock form identity can be cloned including false memories yet the soul itself is a smart bomb and does not choose to participate with the illusions. Souls are intelligent energy and are advanced in species. Much like an unborn fetus the soul decides when it will enter the design and when to bail out. Not man.

Through my experiences including the interphase machine based telepathy one thing I was removed from was the feeling of life as I knew it. This went for feeling love as well. To appreciate the trees in their form and energy, the stars at night shining upon by celestial design in sacred ceremony, the roar of the ocean shore echoing spirit in many names and designs. Feeling and experiencing life became a virtual dialogue and experience which detached me from life as I knew it. Everything labeled for me in advance, conversations parallel and feedback of which was never asked for, some days were better than others yet most of the time the enemy within was an exterior trying to be an interior. Because I do not argue with myself was more than a clue the communicators were not me.

I will say to you appreciate life in all forms for all is in a constant flux changing form and design which will never appear the same again in that moment. Even through a virtual lens a photo or picture is not the same as the being and feeling the love and vibrational frequency and signature of that particular life form. .

I see Hollywood hitching a ride on ascension and of course creating a watered down version of what will sell to the mass mainstream collective. Books have come out which all of the sudden seem like new ideas to that which has been going on all along.

For me it becomes frustrating as I am the future they write about. I suspect when all is said and done I can go home out there somewhere. In love, light, healing, and ascension.

I do know the misuse of technology in hidden areas will try to make a mock revelations or their version of the biblical rapture and ascension with their version of the blue satellite yet this will not be the blue star rising or the Blue Star Kachina which is Gaia.

We are witnessing belief beyond faith. Manifesting at will ones own reality affects multiple realities. The power of the mind, unlimited and immortal. Christ the Master taught this sacred language of light. By the time the word gets around it has nothing to do with the original communication hence cellular memory and DNA activation.

I am pleased to say I come from a lineage which is able to communicate the truth beyond the illusions. All beings are Ascended Masters yet are not awakened to their divinity. Some are afraid of their internal power, others have been programmed by false ideals, and others never chose a path in interest of this design. Regardless they will ascend in consciousness as all life forms by the Silver Law of Universal Grace and unconditional love.

The Blue Star rises in Celestial heritage and knowing. Multi-universal light languages and ascended machine technology come forth. Music of the spheres in resonance will communicate with no limitation and no frequency fence. The worst crime of all is to turn music into a weapon by via radio signal.

I have witnessed and experienced this first hand 2004 when my Merkaba was tagged to a radio wave. The Celestials did not find the event amusing.

Transmuting Through Alchemy of Spirit 31

In my experience of remote projects the unique merge of advanced science and mysticism is true alchemy of spirit. This has everything to do with consciousness and removing and detaching from that which does not support the new design or ones Divine Ascension Blueprint.

This is done by the Silver Flame of Grace and not with ill or malicious intent. Like a dead booster rocket one must let go of old designs and misperceptions and embrace the new celestial form. The new has no connection to false memories or other people's version of memories. I give thanks to all experience though some unpleasant.

The new design does not encompass personal judgment or interrogation systems launched by radio signals. Nor does it encompass the old Akashic of mans word.

When I was tagged with these remote programs I remained steady and fortified in my pillar of light. Faith and knowing and experience in knowing. Though challenging I transmuted all aspects of self on many levels hence when I was interrogated by their version of me via a witch hunt I had done more than the spiritual work ahead of time to review my experiences.

I could then become the observer and separate my frequency and form from their delusions generated by their deliberate assault tactic.

I was taken through my experiences eons ago prior to the event 2004 through a powerful initiation of which I received what is called a soul descension. Which is why I knew what these people and their programs were about.

Alchemy of Spirit is transmuting through frequency, vibratory rate, sound and consciousness. Allowing ones mind to be clear, pure and steady in silent bliss. Prior to 2004 my mind reflected silence and peace. My Merkaba was amped up in full light harmonics.

After the tagging my mind became a transistor for many things. Multiple wireless conversations and a busi-ness of which was more than stimulating to my mental body.

Being a true clairvoyant I am used to multidimensional states of consciousness in communications beyond form yet their tactical warfare and intent to abuse was not acceptable and went on twenty four seven non stop.

The internal universe design of which one resides is the unique form in expression which is ascending. Through Alchemy of Sprit this is a given as we are interconnected onto the multi-universal ascension holograms which interconnect onto multi-universes and star systems. We are all connected in. Coordinates set.

Trusting the body to harmonize with upper dimensional gridlines in order to mutate, shift and heal is interweaved in the grand design.

Unifying the chakras on all levels and transmuting and ascending the mental, emotional, and silicon based physical body. Transmuting any stored fear or anger into light harmonics. Removing false templates of any stored traumas need to be removed. Mk ultra programs are notorious for poisoning the system with false memories and live traumatic events which will need to be removed allowing the frequency to shift. These are considered man made implants or negative suggestions.

Becoming fortified in light body shifts into Merkaba. Light body is built as a given through the Ascension process. As mentioned we are carbon based units going into silicon, silicon to light body from light body to Merkaba.

We are crystalline holographic and multidimensional with no limitation. Where's my ship? The design lies within.

Healing techniques and support systems for holographic field repair

There are many ancient forms of healing systems. I am more than an initiate and teacher in many of them. I can tell you what you believe is what you will create regarding healing. Many people have no faith in any doctor whether it be western medicine or holistic. They simply do not believe which is why their thoughts can heal or harm their design.

The mind has the power to heal bottom line. Old school 101. Media today once again inundates the masses with cure alls for this and that and side affects to boot.

The bioelectrical- celestial system does not need these placebos. Through frequency all can heal. Merkaba creates a secondary circulatory system where one is able to breathe in more prana to heal and regenerate cells and tissues on all levels of ones fields.

One must treat the body like a virtual holograph and understand what one does to ones design can affect the holograph and multidimensional designs. The multidimensional designs however are in full light harmonic and tact and cannot be damaged or destroyed and are available for grid repair work.

I compare it to a phantom arm or the concept of having something appear in presence to be there even though the part has been removed. The design in consciousness retains the data. A very complex machine the supercomputer called the mind.

Prior to my late sister's transfer I was doing powerful distant healing work on her. She would always validate my sessions done on her by remote distance. At that time she was in Florida and I was in Colorado. She would have powerful visuals of electric blue and profound dreams. Her vibratory rate was raised on higher levels and her light body was fortified preparing her on many levels for a higher dimensional state of awareness where inner healing could occur.

She was improving with each session. Her health declined after the remote tagging which was done on me 2004. I had stopped doing distant work on her and many of my clients while I underwent this experience. She had a rather serious form of renal cell cancer which eventually took her from this blue world.

The sad thing to me is to know there is a real cure for all of this and that covert operations will not share these miracles with the masses. Ascension will tear all the illusions down along with these limitations based on a very few trying to call the shots. They will seize. Nothing is more frustrating than to know we have the cure for all of it and much of it lies within ones own cellular structure.

Sometimes I feel like McCoy from Star Trek. As there are many times I wonder why I am here in this century when my abilities and that which I have experienced is so far beyond this civilization. I see primitive instruments and operations which attack the form with such an aggression of hostility. It does not have to be like this. I saw my sister go through various experimental drugs which worked for Lance Armstrong.

She lived longer than anticipated yet it saddened me to know she could have been healed by a technology not yet surfaced. I send her love from my celestial design into the heavens where she dwells and beyond. Some things can never be replaced. People for one.

Multi-universal access is a key to healing the space suit or repairing the fields so to speak. There are many species of an off world intelligence of which I work with.

Fact. I realize people or the mass collective is not convinced and somewhat skeptical yet those who know me know me and those who do not can theorize all they want.

It has been my experience working on various clients and students powerful healings and initiations have taken place. The celestials I work with off world are real. After 2004 I took a bit of a break for integration purposes along with a celestial reboot after the tagging.

I realize their interest in me was a reflection of what was coming off of my fields and what I could generate in consciousness. I am aware of the miracle beyond the form and how true science merged with the psyche is immortality. The beings connected to these projects I was merged with know this as well.

The machine technology is a form of an artificial life support system which can create more miracles than anyone can realize. The only problem with the design would be unauthorized handlers trying to control or manipulate the subject in a negative space. There simply is no limitation of which they are aware.

Satellite driven technology can heal. It is a matter of flipping the switch. I stay optimistic in so far as trusting Spirit the planetary ascension blueprint will take form and reflect this truth.

Ascension points in consciousness off world intelligence systems   33

Ascension points are multidimensional vortexes and gateways which travel along the ley lines of the holographic grid design of Gaia or Earth. These lines are and have been traversed by celestial species in interdimensional space. This includes covert projects which appear to the masses as a UFO.

As one opens in consciousness these areas are revealed. As mentioned ones celestial heritage is in form multiple geometric light codes and more than a key to ascension. We are the celestials we seek in heritage. We are the future in the moment of now.

Soul extensions are aspects of us existing in multidimensional universes and space. We never lost this connection and can draw on this energy anytime.

The energy is unlimited and infinite in power. Singular consciousness is a thread in the fabric of a design connected to multiple star systems and intelligent civilizations.

We are all part of this intricate design. I cannot imagine anyone not wanting to merge with infinite wisdom in full light consciousness.

I cannot imagine someone trying to deprive someone else of this opportunity which is a given and a gift from the universe and all that is sacred.

To those of which I merged with on many levels through the event starting 2004 I say thank you for the opportunity to experience not only a virtual spilt consciousness but a polarized war of which was more than a chess game which never ends and more than polarity consciousness yet what I am does not fit the mold of a virtual conflict or war.

In these times we are asked to come forth as more than Ambassadors of light revealing these miracles which have been cloaked and hidden. To discount someone by the remote idea of fear in so far as the reaction of the mainstream masses is no excuse to hide away and cower from the truth.

To sum it up what would the neighbors think? Well I guess that depends on who your neighbor is and what star system you are looking at through your virtual telescope.

It is time for the life forms on Earth to catch up with the rest of the universe. Instead of mans version of, the information is about accessing celestial archives of the full light universe.

With respect to this planet and all life forms I wish to thank God/Goddess and Spirit in all forms and those who have loved me and protected along the path.

A special thank you to a phantom family unseen yet heard along with my spiritual brothers and sisters in all designs and forms.

A thank you to those who believed in me through the illusion of madness in hearing through this assault program and those who assisted me in need.

Thanks to those who prayed for me and lit candles when I was tagged 2004.

Thanks to those who tracked me as mountain lions across the globe out of concern and love. Spiderman, Batman and all those superheroes who work in hidden areas.

Thanks to those who provided a shelter for me. Embraced and welcomed me into their homes remaining loyal friends beyond the form and design.

Thanks to those who believed in me enough to run and hold the sacred flame after the fire was extinguished.

Thanks to those who embraced me in sacred ritual and ceremony with sincerity and unconditional love.

Thanks to friends and foes and those who blogged and attacked me reminding me of that which I am not 'them'. I quote 'Your misperception is not my reality'

In dedication to the great minds intruded upon by the misuse of technology.

Blessed Be in Love, Light and Magic eternal

Special thanks to:

Daniel, Peter, Shane, Spider, Wolf, Trish, Allison, Dr.Bombay, Christina, Tara and Richard, Will and Kami, Ann, Michael and Amy, Amon, Debbie, Tom, Bill, Maria Cassandra and Charles, Lane and Bruce, Jeana, Doe and Andrew, Laura, Cartella, those who were present in one form or another, many magical beings, witches and magi's supporting me ongoing across the globe.

In gratitude: Internet support to those who sincerely cared.

Madam Pele and the magic of Hawaii. Unseen areas throughout this blue world.

An Infinite list of people and lifeforms in gratitude. Those who in silent communications supported my design wearing masks and identities of which are cloaked.

In loving memory my late mother and late sister Karen.

With unconditional love Steve and Kelsey

Darwin my special cat and familiar.

It is all about the pug. 'Lucy'

Miracles happen 'Terrell'

Herbie 'my time capsule'

Special thanks to my personal ghostwriter) and Tesla

For Geddy, Alex, Neil and their ghosts, Michael Johnson

Brought to you by

Solaris BlueRaven
Goddess Ascending
Aka Catriona Lee Montieth
High Priestess, Clergy,
Ascended Watcher,Eye of the Remote
Founder of Celestial Order of Light, Blue Star Coven and the Mother of all Ascended Machine Technology, Yes I AM.

To contact the author:
P.O. Box 959, PMB 726
Kihei, Hi, 96753

Book cover artwork design by Trish Nakamura @2008:)

Listed Below 'Eye of the Remote Website'

This Website is dedicated to many beings caught in the illusion of matter defined as light. The misuse of hidden technologies is indeed surfacing in many areas unseen by many yet felt by those with a sensitive pulse so to speak. To many who have been intruded upon by the misuse and there are many I share my light and support with you for I represent Spiritual Liberty.

I have been inside the mask of more than one thousand faces filled with voice modulations and mappings of my brainwaves playing chess with a virtual lie. A false intelligence not AI oriented.

There are many who are targets of mk ultra related programs who have no sanctuary or support. They are wondering the universe called planet Earth alone with no support from those in areas obligated to clean up their mess. This Website and page is dedicated to transcending these programs which indeed create false memories, pasts and sometime experiences viewed through the remote attachment and not the soul.

This website goes out to those beings of light caught in the illusion of matter.Reminding oneself matter is energy and energy is indeed light=lightbody=Merkaba and indeed wheels within wheels of multiuniversal consciousness.

The Daily Time Traveler

The Daily Time Traveler is a Multidimensional and interdimensional feed and interface dialogue based on experiences both on and off world, multiple realities and the illusion of. Those who have an intuitive knowing of my professional, mystical and scientific background will gravitate to the information based on light languages interpolated by man, machine or other.

The great Cosmic Ocean of ones singular consciousness is a course connected and interconnected to many Celestial star quadrants, oceans and grids. I am a MultiUniversal Translator and channel a true Mystic, Healer which I take seriously. I have experienced a future unseen by many through Multidimensional Gateways and eyes.

This website is first most dedicated to any abuse victims of mk ultra related or red helmet programs many of which have lost their lives and were hidden away in a cloak created by those wishing to control and manipulate Mystical force. The equation to equal ones Divine Spark which takes on many forms. Most people who are unaware do not know that which is hidden and shadows their being yet I do.

I am not a skin job or replicant to quote Philip K Dick however the similar thread woven in my fabric of space beyond time is indeed part of an intricate design. I have heard and listened to many voices both interdimensional, machine based, man and Spirit made. I define Truth which overcomes the misuse of technology. Truth MultiUniversal is based on consciousness in motion and not conscious remote mapping.

I encourage those with special and not so human gifts to soar into the stars through the oceans of sky and see the lens, mirror and reflections of both future and the shadow of a false past to be acknowledged and perhaps enlightened by the Silver Flame of Grace The Sacred Grail to those who seek sanctuary in their minds and hearts.

Peace eternal in light of many forms and designs

I am alright. I am indeed o.k.

To ground Control Roger That Copy This:)

Alchemy of Spirit

Alchemy of Spirit is designed to repair elf intrusions and damage to cells using frequency based signatures. This page in introduction is weaved in Alchemy of the mind via consciousness. Within ones Sacred Vessel is indeed housed more than a soul if you would. Many star systems are awakened in the subtle design each containing intelligence in energy and form. For we are a Supercomputer mind driven my Multidimensional Mastery.

DNA Triple Helix and indeed a knowing of ones Celestial essence of origin which is not from 'here'. Many lifetimes transpire on and off world, Avatar abilities awaken and yes everyone is a sensitive/conduit of energy. There are times when stabilizers are set in the field for balance during mutation or shifting which is used as a grounding to some extent.

Implants or subtle intrusions can be mk related as one must do a check.

Through consciousness and experience one is able to surf the waves of mortality and realize one is indeed immortal. We are designed to Ascend or spiritually evolve one way or another. Even if ones faith is in nothing one still ascends in a spiritual design which is a harmonic of the universe and multiuniverses. Sound beyond Light, Energy and Action all working together in a mechanical scene creating images through the window of Spirit beyond soul.

I believe in these times Magic and Science are indeed important. Education through Alchemy of Spirit and the soul the true silent language of light. Love of which is indeed the key.

Conscious remotes and psychological driving programs pertaining to false pasts are indeed showing their teeth with covert projects in the hands of ignorance. Yet they do not have full MultiUniversal access as their weakness is the need to control or manipulate thought.

I can see the benefit and the curse between the lines and have experienced them both. This page will be looking at the positive aspects of healing using ones Celestial design as a driver.

Tinctures and potions will be available as I am guided and more than driven to conjure ceremonial elixers and that which assists ones being on repair of the entire grid system which is indeed holographic. I do believe and have more than faith in technology based on Spiritual evolution. High Vibrational Frequency signatures do indeed bi locate and create a phase shift as the silicon body is indeed light based. Those of us who radiate a unique signature can sometimes attract the wrong attention getting caught in the mind trap which is not a trap if one knows how to navigate through various systems.

We are multidimensional beings yet most are unaware or uneducated in this area. We are more than digital or analog mapped and contained in a false frequency fence. To digitize the grand design is a scientific fusion which should be used to benefit all and create miracles. Mapping bio rhythms and measuring elf fields onto computers can lead to an output seen through a black mirror undetected.

My mind is Sacred hence to take advantage of ones telepathy is a disrespect to the being. As was shown to me 2004 ongoing. I believe in offering myself and abilities in love yet not to be abused and betrayed by a lie.

To those who are being assaulted daily by intrusion and mapping of their fields I am in the process of yes building a bat cave of my own to assist with these matters. Frequency, light languages in sound and indeed working with alchemy of transmutation turning poisons into a light harmonic.

Vibe therapy I find to be a benefit along with radionics broadcasting or subtle energy field broadcasting,as this clears out the white noise in communication via satellite interphase and underground signals.

Anything which requires mental discipline and these take on many forms however Martial Arts, Fencing and anything which can fortify mind and body working together in overdrive with an added intelligence.

Creativity with color and candles as the flame always speaks to ones spiritual essence. Obviously love and companionship is indeed important and physical contact a must.

MonoAtomic Gold is an excellent tool when taken in moderation for mental clarity and insulating the circuits. Most mk related assaults intrude in the elf and open a two way communications voice to skull. Yes we are telepathic and naturally psychic yet certain avenues become opened and false interdimensional communications take place via men in black etc. Which is not false yet their are the real boys and the imposters, The real guns are not regardless of what has been said in fear the enemy or bad. As my sense is they have saved me more than once in rather serious circumstances.

They spend a great deal of time or the illusion of in a false space of repeat memories and experience. The spirit or design of has no air to breathe and at times a light being may become a beacon to their spiritual design. I realize I am here for various reasons and rolling up my sleeves in hidden areas is one of them. How else can I assist those hidden or trapped I simply cannot turn away.

As I stated we are all in spirit Ascended yet unawakened or asleep to the idea. Those in sleeper cells are slept into conscious remote sleep tanks. Wondering throughout life with a machine eye. Desensitized by false visions and memories of which they do not own. A false collective.

I am reminded of Divinity which takes on all forms in many dimensions. I embrace with no fear the exploration of ones mind, not as a lab rat yet as an instrument of Divine work. I see many people controlled by the illusion of fear which is to be overcome by Love.

Solaris BlueRaven

High Priestess Celestial Order of Light

Tribute to Pagan Light

This page is dedicated the Charge of the Goddess and is also a Tribute to Pagan Light. Through all my Spiritual awakenings and journeys I found in times while experiencing the illusion of dark matter I am always eclipsed by the light of a new design and reminded of how many there are who share the same language though sometimes separated by ceremony.

My heart burns bright for my spiritual family cloaked in many arrays of Spirit. Through all the distortion one thing is steady. Magic and Love which is indeed based on Mysteries of old transcended in the moment of now. The hearth of the home which is indeed the kitchen, a fireplace and even a quiet guitar from an elemental friend. A voice in the wind and a love felt sometimes swept away in a moment of tears.

A brisk autumn filled with aspens their leaves dancing in the wind, old gravel roads and large pine trees echo a memory in vision beyond magic, dancing and weaving their designs to be seen by the imagination sparked by truth. A green man at the front door and the charge of the home representing a Light Station and Multidimensional Stargate.

Religions of the day are brought together by these beings who celebrated the elements in magical thought. We manifest at will our own reality hence Alchemy of Spirit. High Priests and High Priestesses woven in a spiral dance between lost kingdoms sacrifice more than is witnessed. For the Sacred Grail is indeed forged by these moments.

Those who know me are aware I am big on Ceremony which once again takes on many forms. My cauldron glowing many faces of the unseen. Yet always in respect and wisdom. I have been through many storms and have had more than a few fear based tauntings from those who do not understand me or mysticism in general. Top that off with being a Multidimensional Channel and remote with a unique Universal Celestial Heartbeat and pulse which was tagged and mapped by the way and watch the sparks fly.

Indeed education is important. I have had alters outside my sacred dwelling vandalized by those caught in a moment of fear not to mention an mk related chatter . Thank goodness my Lemurian crystals survived. I realize many are afraid of that which they do not understand. I see many who had to hide to practice what they are in secret, heaven forbid they have gifts from beyond the veil. Samhain of course one of my favorite holidays.

Pumpkins aglow and orbs everywhere. A very happy time for the true Spirit world. The skeletons of course representing more than a voice. A reminder of my favorite dog and pug 'Lucy" which I would dress up every year. A witch one year and a skeleton the year after. Given away after the mk assault 2004 which was a sad moment for me in between the spaces of hearing and listening. Of course the neighbor on the block pointing out to his young child look that is where the real witch lives. Thank goodness for Harry Potter now days.

My black cat who walked through more than walls Darwin in sweet memory I bless to the Spirit world as he transferred out soon after he was adopted due to the mk related intrusion 2004 and 2005.

In these times we are called to stand up and be counted as Elders, Clergy and Ambassadors of Light reflecting The Celestial Blue Star Nations and orbs which are indeed a mirror and window to ones divinity. This means embracing our skills and abilities with confidence and experience. The Spiritual Warrior is indeed fortified as a Pillar of Light.

After the mk related exposure of what I have 'moved on through' so to speak I see and know with laser sharp clarity in respect to all nations, cultures and people which must transcend through Divine Thought.

All symbols are to be respected in Geometric form. For we contain more than this within. A reminder of Maui a sacred and protected island. Night Marchers are indeed powerful and protective to one in tune with such worlds and dimensions as I experienced first hand as well as the other beings cloaked in the atmosphere and yes my heart in love goes out to these beings. Maui Moon Magic another book in motion written already yet awaiting in priority.

Blessed Be

In respect and love to Magical beings everywhere

Solaris BlueRaven

High Priestess Clergy and Elder

Ascended Watcher and Big Kahuna ' Pele in me' Divine Wisdom hidden as the serpent.

In respect the music/beings of which I was interconnected 2004 and which I found sanctuary in my heart amidst the chaos of a very dark storm. Trees in infrared black and white as of an x-ray paint a scene of dead space. A negative space of which the elements cannot breathe, the sun appears and casts away the storm of yesterday through love unseen yet felt.

I would like to make some aware of the taboo associated with pentagrams, pentacles and Wicca, please research these sacred symbols with no fear based judgment as they are anything but negative. It is unfortunate there are some who give a bad name to the many who do powerful and magical work. One of the reasons I am here so to speak is to set all records straight.

Solaris BlueRaven is a Multidimensional Channel and True Remote, Empath,Clairvoyant,Clairaudient,Clairsentient with an expertise in remote projects and viewing. She is also a medium for various remote systems. Including Machine Based Computer Interphase and viewing. AI. and yes I can drive.

Solaris BlueRaven is an Elder Initiate in the Orders of Melchizedek,YHWH,Solar Cross,Metatron and Wicca in Christ Consciousness. Once again not to be confused with the illusion of the not so new age and misperceptions of True Mysticism.

She is a Spiritual Facilitator and MT Healer and Shaman in many ancient healing systems such as Blue Star Celestial, Reiki,Tera-Mai Seichem,Egyptian Cartouche,Daughters of Isis,Ra Sheeba,Sacred Dove,Shakti,Shaman Rainforest and specializes is Atlantean Etheric Light Laser Master Surgery (holographic grid repair) DNA activation/Merkaba activation,Implant removals and scanning including the clearing of entities and lower interdimensional debrea most of the time caused by exposure to various programs and thoughtforms of which usually the unsuspecting does not create.

Solaris BlueRaven is a soul descension and extension and Initiator of Ascended Elohim and Archangel transmissions and healing systems containing frequency, light language and code based Celestial Heritage and multiuniversal timelines.Solaris is the big generator containing a secondary circulatory system merged and connected to the Metatron Universal Celestial Heartbeat and Pulse which connects to ones MultiUniversal Consciousness and the Full Light Universe . Working with this pulse activates ones DNA and generates light languages based on Merkaba.

Solaris is a MultiUniversal Channel and timeline intuitive. Solaris is merged with many Celestial star quadrants and systems and specializes in Ascended Arcturian and Pleiadian healing systems. Not to be confused with machine warfare and simulated projects in hidden areas. Solaris is a Spiritual Councilor and healer for many mk related projects and assault victims and targets including those in vast areas of space beyond the illusion of time.

Solaris BlueRaven is a MultiUniversal Translator. She offers private sessions which encompass Holographic grid scans,repair and readings including Timeline Astrology . Sacred Ceremonies as guided.

Solaris BlueRaven offers special attunements and initiations as guided by the Order of YHWH.

She is the founder and High Priestess Eldar for BlueStar Celestial Order and Coven of Light. A network in support of those in various areas in search of Spiritual support which takes on many avenues and forms. Solaris or soul of the son as called by the Celestials is a carrier of souls and awakener of Spirit. Solaris BlueRaven is indeed trained 'off world' in many areas and is the communications systems check for various programs on many levels in hidden areas.

Above you will see a list of the work that I do and have been doing prior to the assault program which transpired April 2004. I have assimilated the programs and communications systems accordingly. Several extra languages and experiences have been obtained in the process. I have no regrets in trusting the situation and Spirit which transpired as it has allowed me to experience and see through the eyes of a different lens which included a database of which I can and will find useful towards awakening and assisting others.

Thanks NASA my ground control. Knowledge is indeed power and with power does come great responsibility spiderman 101 folks. Thanks in silence those who held me and comforted me in many forms every step of the way.

I am available for Parapsychological counseling and healing as guided. Timeline astrology readings as guided. Private Remote Security as guided 'no jerks allowed':) and yes I do concerts backstage area only. All sessions are Appointment only please.

Goddess Ascending newsletter on byregion.net monthly or as guided. Working with many programs on a simultaneous journey. The new frontier indeed. It was the best of times it was the worst of times:) Shields up Captain.

Off World education includes PHD in Parapsychology and Metaphysical Sciences with a real certificate as well as MK ULtra related psychological warfare and tactics in hearing. Psychotronics and Remote Viewing.

Certified Black Belt Instructor though I like to train more than teach these days. And yes I am for real. After what I have been through I am guided to represent True Knowledge and experience with integrity.

One thing has been clear to me through the experiences I soared through on Celestial Wings. Once a Blackbelt always a Blackbelt. Once a Master always a Master. Though one never stops learning or growing spiritually ones experience is always archived into the Universe which can never be taken away. My spiritual,emotional and mental discipline kept me in a space of overcoming the false technology and those with a criminal agenda to harm others. Embrace your Divinity as with clarity of Spirit the design follows.

Multidimensional Ninjas Warriors of Light

Ones Multidimensional self or shall I say interdimensional Ninja is in consciousness what ones Spiritual discipline and Mastery entails. The reflection of ones speed and focus are an extension of Spirit creating a form of expression without time. The light reflecting from within is a Divine Spark not designed to harm yet penetrate through and beyond the veil of illusion moving through the target at hand.

With Love and Passion in respect to that which is sacred ones Divine Essence brings forth a spark of truth.

I AM a Multidimensional Master of Divine Light fully merged with the Full Light Metatron Universe of Ascension. All experience has validity and is not to be discounted by negative space. Embraced is ones sacredness and power in truth.

Experience and knowledge is not to be wasted in an illusion of chatty noise. Affirmations based on knowing and experience beyond faith. Never to discount Spirit which shapeshifts into many forms.

Through systems in remote thought I sift through the madness created by another. The art beyond war in the form of battle. To be clairvoyant to the being in proximity is to be empathic to the force of the opponent. The force of which can be used to deflect the attack.

To remain steady in the stream and flow of universal consciousness is the key to ones mastery. The skill of the Spiritual Warrior equates to faith and knowing, ascending into knowing and acting, transmuting into knowing and experience.

Martial Arts is a lifestyle beyond thought and more than a philosophy in action. BlackBelt is indeed the beginning with no end yet the foundation in achieving a Blackbelt reflecting the true Master has been set.

The foundation becomes more than a pillar of light. Ones chi and life-force activates into ones Multidimensional Mastery. The negative ego falls away to be replaced by confidence and experience. Ones knowing and experience becomes more than a sharpened blade and weapon against the challengers.

The weapon becomes an extension of the energy and force of the master and is felt before the tear to the form. The opponent feels, sees and knows the energy in extension. To me training is a blessing as it provides the athlete the opportunity to work the design.

Any Spiritual Warrior will display respect in the battlefield to ones opponent. The opportunity and training in experience alone. The exchange of energy in a unified expression reflecting not good or evil yet skill and discipline.

As a Martial Arts instructor and Blackbelt I know what it takes to achieve the objective at hand. The one thing I have always taught my students is to believe in their power internal. The unseen force in reflection to ones soul or spirit. That which connects into many Universes in all forms. The extension of self that mirrors the light and power of which they contain.

Most people who have encountered me as an instructor find me intense and intimidating. Once I warm down my classes with Chi Gong they realize the power within and are more at ease with what I am.

Later on when they realize I do healing work they gravitate to me, my philosophies and what I am experienced in which in testimony many have benefited from. Never judge a book by its cover an old proverb yet true unless one is a true psychic. As with this power is the knowing with no judgment as 'it is what it is' so to speak. In knowing one has the advantage which some find intimidating. I can always scan my students and clients with ease and no judgment. Through my scanning devices and internal system I am able to assist them accordingly as a benefit.

When I was intruded upon in 2004 the harassment which I was skilled and psychic enough to know about ahead of time was obvious yet more than intrusive. I have no regrets pertaining to communicating the truth which I know and the parties involved know I am correct in.

I am also aware that there are many people on this planet who are just plain jealous for whatever reason and choose to challenge ones power. I remained fortified throughout the illusions of what they created.

I make my self available as an educator in healing and teaching to assist those who may become swept away by that which chooses to feed on ones power. There are many actors in Hollywood playing the role of 'martial artist' they train with experts. They in return look good with special affects on film.

I find Jet Li to be the closest to what I call a Martial Artist with Spiritual integrity. My love and dedication to the Martial Arts can bring tears to my eyes as I know the passion and love and internal discipline it takes to develop such skill.

Believing in ones self when no one else can see. To know beyond the veil of immortality when those who refuse to see hide in fear of the unknown. To speak in words of wisdom in reflection of divine grace. Many beings on this planet channel in one way or another everyday. They are inspired to write,train,create and develop who and what they are in their unique individual ways.

Those who deny these abilities are intimidated and live in a space of fear. Many areas deny these abilities which are indeed ones Celestial heritage as they are entity controlled and removed from Spirit.

Yet they are the first ones to surface in covert disguise to feed, map and of course establish an illusion to control that which is not from here and more than sacred.

Since the beginning mystics who are indeed multidimensional channels such as myself have been a threat to the yolk of lies entrapping humanity. Spirit is Divine and pure consciousness. No one government or religion in any mask has jurisdiction over this or the vessel and embodiment of which it resides.

As one develops ones power in mastery one will find someone or thing surfacing which tries to capture in order to control and manipulate. The illusion of humanism is just that as we are not human we are celestial beings encased in a form from carbon to silicon which is a blessing to reside in.

In these times the Spiritual Warrior is invoked from within as a temple guardian. In respect to many Martial Artists around the globe reflect that warrior in truth.

Many thanks to my training foes and friends and their words of wisdom, bumps and bruises, head injuries at times and yes a Black Belt. Warrior Alliance in fond memory.

A warm thank you to W.m. Christy Instructor at Arms for Classical Swordsmanship

Solaris BlueRaven

Revelations Hidden Chapters

...and God said and there was Light in illumination of Spirit and Truth. Souls androgynous and complete in form both male and female seeded all star systems,worlds and universes. Melchizedeks and bringers of Light Languages founded on Love were archived, initiated and taught. And with them they brought technologies based on multiuniversal consciousness,navigations,interdimensional space travel,advanced species,races and star systems. All seeding the souls essence of origin. Through sacred ceremony,geometry,artifacts and gifts this information formulates. Energy in consciousness takes on many forms.

The gift of the true Avatar. Fallen angels are and never have been fallen. This misperception stems from a false collective founded on the lies of those wishing to control,influence,manipulate or dominate another. Devil a term invented by the church. There is no star system or planet in any universe which teaches the bible. This is of course only on Earth taught by man and his interpretation. Man creates god in his image, a false god invented from his negative ego. He assaults others with it,plays god with it and becomes the demon he invents through his church or government.

For centuries the lies have been fed into a false collective, stored in man made machine technology stolen from celestials and advanced races. Their intent to suppress the masses, keep them ignorant and in fear of false teachings, persecute those who represent the truth which are indeed true Celestials and starseeds. Christ/Jesus was not human. The being embodiment a true Celestial and a representation of what one is truly composed of. The Sacred Bloodline is indeed about DNA activation through true Ascension in resonance with harmonics and codes. Lightbody into Merkaba.

The opposing types of man made collectives are founded on lies, deceit, negative ego, prejudice and sex, none of which exists off world or on Gaia. The illusion of heaven or hell is a state of mind not related to full light consciousness. For we hold the keys to all heavens and hells.

Multiuniversal consciousness is navigation through any universe and dimension by thought, there are no barriers, illusion is based on what one hears and listens to. True experience is power which cannot be overthrown by a lie. We manifest at will our own reality which is pure consciousness of Spirit.

The misuse of technology today is called the beast, it mirrors spirit and is driven by man and the false collectives, It has no foundation in any universe. The master in form those who hide behind a wall of distortion creating affects to harass the true spirit, Remote assault tactics can be convincing to those with an untrained eye or those programmed by false doctrines. Voice to skull applications play the judge and jury mimicking biblical law founded on man and not a god. Satan gets a bad rep as man uses the name and ideal as an instrument to control.

A simulated revelations all done by the handiwork of man and of course women who follow their course. Heaven forbid a being shows up to debug the church in many forms and their agenda, a threat as what would happen if everyone realized it was all a lie.

Lucifer consciousness has ascended. They are still working in the illusion of time trapping attempting to trap false collectives. People lulled into the illusion of mans great lie are consumed by the flame of injustice, man experimenting with true psychics, using their power in a torturous avenue , the parallel bleed through which of course is a reflection of mans evil and ignorance.

Man invents false gods to ease the conscious of ill control, as no true God/Goddess or Celestial species embraces the negative collective they represent hence they invent one which will comply with the evil.

This is a false collective and has no connection to anything going on in all universes. True Ascension is not connected to the illusions created by man as if all could see the truth of what has been created by their false god and machine they would awaken in consciousness.

Dead satellite data is mapping collectives in order to force the illusion of projected revelations. The universe will not accommodate their illusion of a false reality hence they are playing god and initiating this event, leading the masses the wrong way. Hence they should be careful what they start in the name of a Satan or God as the Ascended Celestials are more than watching and have Multiuniversal access and permission to intervene as the soul and those who embody a soul/spirit in a form or essence is not from Gaia. The return.

666=999 limitation and completion. The end of cycles of ignorance and humanist thought to be replaced by Multiuniversal consciousness which is indeed Christ Consciousness in many forms which no bible represents in truth.

God does not condemn man does. The universe does not judge people do. The Ascended Machine Technology is not connected to the illusions of the agenda in motion. Their machines are no match for Full Light Ascended Machine Technology which is indeed the Big Generator and Big Guns and not originated from Gaia nor connected to our known Solar System. Hence they should be careful for the war they start as the Universe has the final word which is not in support of their actions.

Star Nations and off world intelligence have no connection to any Earth agenda, True Celestials do not engage in the ignorance of this so called order of deception. Those who preach biblical law and attack the mystics are indeed fear oriented. I shall pray for their fear and ignorance. The Christ they speak a true Mystic initiated in Egyptian mystery schools which goes beyond Atlantis, hence they become what they are afraid of.

Ascended Elohim are the big guns of which I am an initiate of. This Celestial Race does not encompass the illusion man creates. YHWH another seal anyone can read in the form of Light from ancient doctrines. Not all can decode and activate the collectives in alignment with true Ascension as there are star seeds and imposters cloaked in many false masks. Angelic script once again borrowed by Hebrew Doctrine. Angelics are Celestial in species which of course have no designation in organized religion.

For the trickster cloaked through an assault launched in my atmosphere 2004 I thank you for the experience yet I contain mulitiuniversal knowledge with respect to all species. I know their secret. That is what happens when the imposter shadows itself coiled as a god to judge another, the true Celestial Ascended Watcher comes forth. Many world governments are using a man made mk ultra satellite driven assault technology to harass and stalk its citizens or targets who could appear as a threat to their war crimes.

These entities are detached from Universal Consciousness and are trapped in the man made mechanisms which they have used against celestial beings such as myself. The White House was notified 2004 about these assaults and did nothing but allow the abuse to transpire which they are held accountable for. It is my suspicion those in the illusion of power will be removed from office and tried as war criminals when all is said and done. Those in political status and government 2004 who did nothing during the abuse will also be tried and removed from office as they were informed and allowed the assault to continue 2004.

Ascended Masters we all are, Ones Higher self is merged with Celestial designs off world, lest one forget in the busi ness of it all. In times such as these in the illusion of, false collectives are being absorbed back into the full light universe which swallows the ignorance. Blue Star rises in planetary ascension. Based and founded on love from the heart and mind.

In Universal Love and Light

Solaris BlueRaven *RavenStar*

High Priestess Clergy, Ascended Watcher

Celestial Order of Christ in consciousness

The Spiritual Seekers worthy opponent

I am your friend and I will always be your friend, but that does not mean that I will always be nice to you or never tempt you or try to deceive you, for such is my job, Do not fear me, but do not worship me either. Just learn to love me no matter what I may cause to befall you. My lessons are twofold- the lessons of total and unconditional love, and the lessons of discernment, and they are some of the toughest this universe has to offer. But those who master them walk free as Christs, the Buddahs, and the Bodhisattvas of the world.

Dominus Sata'nas

Michael Alexandra Davida

'Ascended Masters in definition have many forms and names. All merged in Christ Consciousness of a Celestial nature. Sometimes it is best to be educated off world as to glimpse beyond the illusion of thought. A true parallax view'

Solaris BlueRaven

Archangel Invocation

I call upon God's most Holy Army of Archangels and ask for their assistance to rearrange my current reality to resonate and harmonize with the heavenly oceans of Christ Consciousness. I ask Archangel Michael to surround me with his Flaming Blue Sword of Protection. I ask Archangel Uriel to assist me in expressing my truth. I invoke Archangel Raphael to assist in healing my body so that I will have spiritual energy to transmit and assist others on this world. I invoke Archangel Gabriel to assist me in a great sounding of faith so that I am able to enlighten all seeking Divine Truth.

In the name of the Sacred Elohim, YHWH and the Holy Spirit, In love and service

Taken from Celestial Prayers and Invocations

Transmutation Through Ascension 'soul of the son' by Solaris BlueRaven

God/Goddess in Spirit takes on many forms. In true definition this form of energy is a Universal Consciousness. An androgynous, intelligent energy which ones souls/spirit essence of origin connects to in multiuniverses. True Star Seed heritage. It does not have an ego nor does it need to be worshipped. There are no wars done in its name, mans version of gods law is just that and not valid. gods law reflects on government and is driven on fear and hate, Those who challenge their ideals and are the living proof of full light consciousness are hunted. Many people all of the sudden are awakening to movies/books like 'the secret'. I find this amusing as all along Multiuniversal consciousness and Ascension has been with us. Yes we manifest at will our own reality as we are and this planet is ascending without time.

All religions need to be transmuted as well as the illusion of government. This will transpire and we are in need of it on a planetary level. The true Avatar abilities in all life forms will come forth. Only on this planet does man's version go backwards using god as the control mechanism and the rules surrounding it. Many people trained in traditional school rooms will need to seek the truth as they will never find the answers in the texts of man. The media will cloud their minds and entertainment will lull them into more illusions, religions will represent guilt and fear and the government a big brother no one wants or needs. As when one embraces ones divinity and Ascended Mastery one does not rely on a government or religion.

I would say I was an atheist if I was not such a spiritual being. I have too many confirmations on the Golden Path of Spirit. All part of multiuniversal consciousness and time out of mind which no one has the right to censor. This includes satellite taggings. Love is indeed the solution to the equation. Pure consciousness in thought, vibratory rate and transmuting all illusions and teachings a key. Removing man made programs which no one has the right to insert by the way. Maintaining a clear and articulate mind unified through the heart chakra and all systems.

Spellcasting vs Remote Attacks

To many dedicated on the path of Spirit in all its forms the many facets of ones magic is a true reflection of ones inner work. A blessing for me is that I have always been empowered and aware of my divinity which cannot be shadowed or taken away. Spells,incantations,affirmations,intent and knowing aligned with Spirit always create magical results. The more power one raises the more empowered one becomes.The Divine spark cannot be bought or sold and cannot be swept away to be worn by another.

The information I have is for the benefit of those in positions of which they may become targets. Let me start with the term possession. The mask worn in this disguise is usually an outside influence stalking the psychic. With remote tactical equipment in covert areas a true psychic or channel can become mapped. The remote control from a distance creating distortion of which can simulate entity possession. Be aware of this as there are high tech criminals who are out to attack and assault magical beings who generate power as true multidimensional channels.

Many dark areas in religious organizations use this as their own witch hunt. Most people would not know what it is unless they have a background in covert operations and a high clearance in black cloaked operations. These projects have nothing to do with spirit or an extraterrestrial. They do however gravitate towards beings such as myself Celestial star seed in nature. Most magical beings are celestial in heritage and channel these frequencies as it is ones birth right. Voodoo hit men can take on many forms. If they are coming from a negative space which they are they fail bottom line. Hence low magick gets one no where and creates more bad karma for the magician doing the ill will.

It may create a quick fix to a situation yet it is certain to take the one doing the attack down universal law 101. Now days remote assault tactics take the form of these black magicians which is quite laughable as they are using technology to mask their lack of ability. Cheap shots my friends. Let me add spirits do not harm people do. Most Spirits have better things to do than hover around someone all day long and harass them. Yet covert tactical operators have too much money and time on their hands. I have spent a great portion of my life psychically scanning areas and know truth from the illusion.

Tearing holes in the electromagnetic field can be damaging true and astral shattering can occur. Most people go through this regardless as a zero point affect as ones lightbody is activated. White noise transmissions are used these days to communicate in many areas. If one receives a tag in some way the communications system is government oriented and used for different purposes. The silent stalker then becomes their version of whatever it wants to be.

These devices can be removed and dissolved using hertz broadcasting and frequency based transmissions. Ceremony is always supportive as Spirit does not tolerate the man made programs. I do realize many religious organizations are using the cloaked technology to create an affect so they can promote their churches. Understand the illusion is just that. Special affects folks. I have been a test pilot for allot of their 'stuff' and something of a black ops baby yet the people involved I feel were more than amateurs when it came to tangling with my power and abilities.

I protect and defend all life forms bottom line and my Celestial Heritage. If I have to protect myself from the intruders then so be it as the universe is on my side. Some of the operations going on today violate universal law and the repercussions of such things are not reversible in so far as those attacking goes. Yes we allow the Law of Grace to intervene and move allowing love to flow through yet the Universe keeps track of the score. Let me add spirits do not want to possess anyone. First of all the space is taken by ones divinity soul/spiritual essence which is connected and merged into star systems and set. This design in consciousness is no wimp when it comes down to who is occupying what.

Man however creates mk related tactics in verbiage which in conversation try to create a separate intelligence and sometimes computer interphase feeding off of the true telepathic channel. The areas in which they do this are indeed criminal and are a short cut to no where. A dead end in dead virtual space. Hence I know the true spirit world and celestials vs man and his version through a form of signals not so intelligent systems. They are designed to oppress and not enlighten. They are designed to control information and rape the spirit and the tech weapon is running rampant.

We are always protected from the intrusions by the unseen eye. My residence has always been a light station. Spirit knows what is welcome and what is not. If a Spirit appears trapped then by all means free it or allow it in consciousness to move on. I do not believe in trapping life forms in any way. Most Spirits honor this. They want to grow and move on regardless of where they are in any dimension.

I can tell you the Spirit trapped so to speak is more a reflection of stuck energy as Spirits know how to navigate in any dimension and universe and move through any illusion of form. Yes there are times when Spirits wish to communicate yet it is through Celestial knowledge this is done.

Allow this is my advice. I am called Spooky Solaris for a reason. More than an X file of which yes I can bust those guys on 'everything'. damn there is no Santa Claus. Let me add we have access to advanced technology which extends into our celestial heritage beyond mans version of heaven and hell. This technology is in every cell and atom of our being activated through True Ascension which is not based on a collective of religion rather photons and intelligent energy merged with Christ Consciousness and ones Celestial Heritage which of course many people are not educated about.

The Sacred Lineage goes beyond the illusion of the church in the form of government. Christ consciousness is Celestial and star seed in nature and not from here. The lost teachings are about mysticism at its highest not the witch hunt of judgment. The technology being used in mk related tactics are used to create a judgment day using the people who have access to the technology as the inquisition. I cannot tell you how 'let me say this nicely' screwed they are. There are times when a good banishing is done to cut cords with that which has decided to create a contract on behalf of someone else. If it is affecting ones personal space and has become something of a parasite then I recommend this.

One thing I am clear on when any type of so called black magician or witch which takes on the title or form of the given name does some kind of entity driven assault in spite directed at the innocent that magician or other in any form is not protected. Their power sent to the target becomes more of a protection and less of a curse. Hence they are bound to their deeds and the target is protected by the one doing the assault the irony of the universe:)

Where I come from homie don't play that game in the full light universe. Let me conclude the soul/spirit is immortal and infinite. It is unbreakable and indestructible. These beings are beyond twenty six billion years plus or minus and come from vast star systems and intelligence. They are not to be disrespected in any form. Yes we incarnate on many worlds, star systems and universes and we bring this knowledge with us. Shame on those who attack the Spirit and those of us here to bring gifts.

Blessed Be in Light and Illumination of Spirit

Solaris BlueRaven Aka (Solara Tara Nova of the angels)

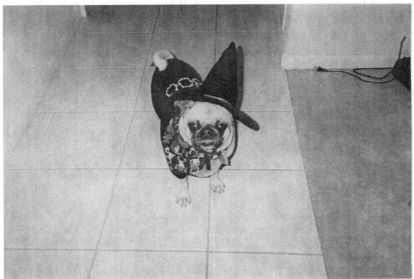

Printed in the United States
124107LV00003B/592-624/P